Unleash the Beast In You - Go from Good to Great

Unleash the Beast In You - Go from Good to Great

THE EIGHT PILLARS OF OPTIMUM PERFORMANCE (EPOP)

Jeff Freeman MBA, PMP

ISBN: 1507600194
ISBN 13: 9781507600191
Library of Congress Control Number: 2015900892
CreateSpace Independent Publishing Platform
North Charleston, South Carolina

Table of Contents

EPOP™

I f just being good is not good enough and being great is your ultimate goal, then this book was designed with *you* in mind. The Eight Pillars of Optimum Performance (EPOP™) is a winning, focused performance-enhancement system consisting of eight corresponding and balanced performance principles designed to help *you* reach your maximum potential. These eight principles work together in harmony using a balanced approach to help you reach the most comprehensive, holistic, continuous, and consistent optimum performance in work, business, school, sport, and home activities.

*EPOP™ is designed to bring out and awaken the beast in **you!***

Jeffery...I'm Disappointed in You

Richard was one of the most knowledgeable men I've ever known. If you asked him a question about any subject matter, he always seemed to have the correct answer. He was also one of those old-school African American men who had been through a lot and had seen some "stuff." He was tough, direct, and maybe a little rude and rough around the edges sometimes. So when I needed real mentorship and guidance, I knew I could get it straight from him.

Back when I was a young lad, about nineteen or twenty years old, I found myself with a dilemma. I didn't go directly to college because I wanted to work with my father in the mortgage business. I thought that by working with him and forgoing college, I would become a young millionaire. However, things didn't go as planned, and the mortgage business happened to be the worst industry to be in at that time. Mortgage rates were 21 percent, and prospective clients needed to be at their jobs for seven straight years in an environment where unemployment was at record highs.

Needless to say, my father's mortgage company didn't last that long, and I was soon working in various odd jobs such as cashiering, selling insulation door-to-door, and finally as a vehicle smog inspector. In addition, I was going to an uncertified, unglorified, boring technician school. I was soon fed up with this seemingly "going nowhere" path, and I thought that a change was in order.

One day, my friend Gary and I decided that we would enlist in the US Air Force, and then, after we finished in the air force, we would become California Highway Patrol (CHP) officers. We decided to go to the air-force office the next day to sign up. So that evening after work, we approached Richard with our plans, hoping to get the final endorsement and support we needed.

Richard was relaxing on his favorite sofa in the living room, drinking what looked like a very strong, brownish adult beverage. He invited us to sit with him, and then he listened to our plans. After we went on for about fifteen minutes, we paused to hear his thoughts. I couldn't wait to hear his admiration.

Richard sighed and looked me straight in the eyes. He jiggled the ice in his glass slightly to make sure it thoroughly chilled the mystery drink. He took another sip from the glass, and in a high and slightly intoxicated voice, he uttered a comment that I would never forget for the rest of my life: "Jeffery, Jeffery, Jeffery, *I'm disappointed in you.*"

I was shocked! I said, "Richard, why are you disappointed in me? I'm working forty-two hours a week, and I'm going to school."

He went on to explain, "You are wasting your life away at that stupid job and going to that dumb school. You should quit that good-for-nothing job tomorrow, stop going to that wretched school, and enroll in a real engineering college."

That was the day I realized that I needed to go from average or good to being great. I realized I had a greater beast inside me that I was not exploring. On that very day, Richard unleashed the beast in me.

Introduction: Unleash the Beast in You!

Think, for a second, about the last "results-oriented" activity you accomplished (e.g., an exam, job interview, presentation, golf tournament, term paper, 5K run, poker game, baking contest, and so on). Did you really do your best? I'm not asking if you did *the* best; I'm asking if you did *your* best.

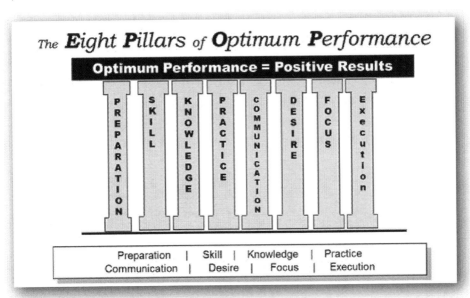

The **Eight Pillars** of **Optimum Performance**

Optimum Performance = Positive Results

P R E P A R A T I O N | S K I L L | K N O W L E D G E | P R A C T I C E | C O M M U N I C A T I O N | D E S I R E | F O C U S | E x e c u t i o n

Preparation | Skill | Knowledge | Practice
Communication | Desire | Focus | Execution

For example, did you make *preparation* paramount to your success? Did you thoroughly assess your *skill set*, and adjust where necessary? And with the skill-set assessment, did you deem your skills appropriate to compete at an optimum level? Were *knowledge* resources and assistance (such as training, tutoring, instruction, and coaching) fully utilized? During this results-oriented activity, did you *practice* extensively, continuously, and exhaustively until you could practice no more?

If you did indeed do your best in the above areas, did you *communicate* the progress of this activity to your support circle of friends, relatives, and colleagues to help ensure you had the right support structure engaged to help you succeed? Of course, you had the necessary *desire* to get you through the tough times. Hopefully, you were able to maintain the necessary *focus* and limit the distractions in your environment.

Finally, and most importantly, when it counted, when it came time to actually *execute* your activity, did you nail it? Did you get the results you wanted? Did you deliver?

If you didn't get the desired results, you most likely did not perform the above steps optimally and in a balanced manner. The above steps work together to make up a performance strategy called the Eight Pillars of Optimum Performance, or EPOP™. The EPOP™ strategy is simple. For any results-oriented activity, ensure you thoroughly concentrate on performing on each pillar optimally. When you achieve high performance in each pillar, you increase the likelihood that you will achieve maximum results in the overall activity. Once you reach this level, you have reached the optimum-performance level in EPOP™—or, in other words, you are in "beast mode." When you are in this mode, you are ready to unleash the beast in you.

However, you will not achieve beast mode unless you reach optimum-performance level on all of the pillars. For example, if the Preparation Pillar is at optimum performance but the Practice Pillar is not, then you will not achieve beast mode. Imagine you complete all the necessary elements to prepare for a major exam, such as planning, organizing, and goal setting. What if, after all the preparation, you didn't take the appropriate time to actually practice for the exam? The chances that you would perform at your best are unlikely and remote. This is not to say that you wouldn't do well in this exam; you might. However, with the EPOP™ method, you can achieve an even better and more consistent top-tier performance and potentially a higher score on the exam. This is why it is important to concentrate on *all* the pillars—so that you maximize your chances for success.

This book was developed to help people achieve consistent, desired results in specific activities as well as daily ones. By subscribing to the EPOP™ strategy and pushing your performance into beast mode, you will unleash the beast in you!

CHAPTER 1

Good Is *Not* Good Enough

n these challenging, unstable, and unpredictable economic times, it is imperative that you know how to deliver, produce, and execute in your job, at school, in sports, or wherever you want to succeed. Not only do you need to produce, but you need to produce when the "lights are on," when the pressure is on, and when all eyes are on you, otherwise known as "game time" or "game on." This is the when it counts—when you give the presentation, make the speech to an audience of hundreds of people, take the test, or play in the game.

In order to have the confidence to perform during these "game-on" times, you need to ensure you complete the proper success components such as preparation, skill, and knowledge, and have the attitude and confidence to finish. However, to do your best in these activities, you can't approach them by just being good or slightly above average—you need to strive for greatness. You need to have an attitude that good simply is *not* good enough.

Once you have these elements in place, you will be more equipped to handle "game-on" situations, which will give you a greater chance for success. This ability to finish, execute, and close out tasks is usually the difference between winning and losing, failure and success, achieving your goal or falling short.

Here in Southern California, where I reside, we are fortunate to have a fabulous hamburger chain called In-N-Out Burger, where their heavenly burgers taste like they subscribe to the theory of "good is not good enough." All of their burgers, but especially the famous Double-Double*, surpass good—they're great! From the first bite down to the grudging last bite, one can tell that In-N-Out has out to create more than just a good hamburger: they are making "beastly" burgers.

Now, since In-N-Out has been around a lot longer than this book, I can't claim that the In-N-Out founders built their burger strategy using EPOP™ principles. But it seems like their burger-building and Double-Double® strategies mirror the EPOP™ principles, leading to a great-tasting, lip-smacking, finger-licking set of burgers. First, just as their slogan states, "Quality you can taste," this double-patty, double-cheese masterpiece starts with painstaking *preparation* (Pillar One). All the burgers (and fries) are prepared with quality in mind. The Double-Double®—complete with lettuce, tomato, pickles, grilled or raw onions, special spread, all together on a freshly baked bun—shows how In-N-Out takes preparation seriously.

Regarding *skill* (Pillar Two), since there are no heat lamps, freezers, or microwaves on the premises, In-N-Out burger specialists need to be a bit more skilled and crafty than the employees at other burger joints. In addition, In-N-Out is *knowledgeable* (Pillar Three) about what it takes to deliver quality burgers to its demanding customers at affordable fast-food prices. The manner in which the Double-Double® is served—with an emphasis on quality yet at a fast and efficient pace—displays the level of training and *practice* (Pillar Four) that is instilled in every employee at every step in the process.

Communication (Pillar Five) is a key component to In-N-Out's success, as they carefully explain their "simple" menu with their slogan, communicating that their strategy is to deliver great burgers and not an exhaustive list of subpar products. The message is simple: You want a great burger? Come to In-N-Out. If you want something else, then perhaps you should go somewhere else.

Also, In-N-Out shows its *desire* (Pillar Six) to stick to what works and not compromise integrity. In-N-Out has one *focus* (Pillar Seven): burgers and fries. The only serve burgers, fries, and drinks, so they can focus efforts on making a high-quality patty. Finally, the *execution* (Pillar Eight) lies in the results of the Double-Double® and all the other burgers: a fantastic burger experience *every time*. In-N-Out, where good is not good enough.

Simply put, always go for better than good, and aim to produce and finish your objectives, or someone else will. Just being good, working hard, and having a good smile will no longer be enough to get by. You need to outperform, *period*. You need to get positive results. You need to be great, because good is not good enough.

CHAPTER 2

Best Equals Beast

Due to layoffs, price pressures, and cost-cutting initiatives in all fields and genres, many people are stuck doing the job of two, three, and sometimes four people with an expectation of no lag in performance. Characteristics such as gender, race, sexual orientation, religion, cultural beliefs, and age are no longer the predominant factors when building teams, partnerships, groups, and companies. Moreover, business and corporate leaders are looking for talented people anywhere and everywhere who will deliver the goods and services and get positive results with few excuses and complaints. Additionally, these leaders want this talent at the cheapest cost possible.

For this reason, "emerging" countries and geographical regions like China, India, eastern Europe, South America, and even Africa are becoming havens in which to find a productive workforce economically. Thus, Americans are not only competing against themselves and western Europe for top talent but also against these emerging regions that produce top performers for minimum cost.

This is why you must be a producer, performer, and results-oriented beast and not a complainer or someone with plenty of excuses. Now is the time to produce positive results in everything you do. Now is the time to execute and *finish*. This is a powerful yet simple statement. Despite all the managerial, organizational, and leadership skills you might have, despite all the education, despite all the good looks and expensive clothes, all that really matters is that *you must perform*.

In short, you must finish the job—you must execute. In order to be successful at any level, you, your team, and your company must perform. In order to "just perform," you must get positive results. There is *no substitute* for top performance. Although hard work and effort are key attributes to success, they are not substitutes for performance. Therefore, it is not about how much you or how long you work; rather, it's about whether you achieve or exceed the set goals in the expected time frame.

The objective of this book is to help you optimize your performance and become a top performer and finisher in whatever you do: business, school, or sports. It doesn't matter what field you're in; everything you do warrants optimal performance to produce results. This book will help you get better results from your efforts.

This book will provide eight proven power principles that will help you build a consistent winning optimal-performance strategy, attitude, and personality. It is important to understand that in order to be a consistent optimum performer and finisher, one must have a balanced and well-planned attack.

It amazes me that most people think that in order to be a top performer, the most important attribute is skill or ability. While these are certainly important, becoming a consistent and balanced optimal performer involves many components.

When you look at great sports performers such as Michael Jordan, Tiger Woods, Diana Taurasi, Sidney Crosby, Derek Jeter, Michael Phelps, Roger Federer, and Serena Williams, they each have several components that make them outstanding performers besides their obvious skill. These include intense preparation, proper training and coaching, willingness to practice for extended periods of time, extreme desire or passion for their sports, and the ability to focus on the task at hand and limit the distractions.

In addition, one common element these top performers share is that they have learned to execute and get positive "winning" results in their respective areas. All these great performers have reached the ultimate performance measurement of winning championships, MVPs, and gold medals. It is their abilities to combine all these attributes into consistent, winning behavior that provides them with dependable opportunities to win.

Top performers are not limited to the sports arena but are found in other industries as well. Some nonathletic top performers include Oprah Winfrey, Meryl Streep, and James Cameron in entertainment, as well as Bill Gates, Steve Jobs, and Jack Welch in the business world. These top performers have produced gigantic positive results in their respective fields for their fans, stakeholders, and investors.

For twenty-plus years, Oprah has continued to produce extraordinary results in revenue and awards for her vast media empire of television, movies, books, and magazines. Year after year, Meryl Streep is either nominated for or the winner of movie awards such as the Oscars or Screen Actors Guild awards. James Cameron has produced and directed two of my all-time favorite movies, *Avatar* and *Titanic*. Not coincidently, these movies are numbers one and two respectively for all-time movie sales, grossing several billion dollars each.

Bill Gates has been a fixture in our lives since the late eighties as the creator of Microsoft. His company produces software products (mainly Microsoft Windows) that have become interwoven in our daily lives. In fact, I wrote this book using Microsoft Windows and Microsoft Word, Excel, and PowerPoint.

Of course, top performers are not just multibillionaires. Most top performers are found in everyday life in your neighborhood, local organizations, communities, local sports teams, and business relationships. Using sports as an example, in basketball it doesn't matter if a player can dribble the ball through the legs and around the back. If that player can't get the ball in the basket, all that talent is wasted effort. In the world of acting, attending acting school for several years does not make someone a top-performing actor. That person needs to audition, win the part, and then nail the performance in order to be a true performer. And there are many more similar examples. This is not to say that basic skills are not important to becoming successful, because they are. However, just knowing the basic skills and participating in the activity will not lead to execution and a results-oriented attitude.

One day early in my consulting career, I participated in an exhaustive performance review with one of the partners. The report was good. I met the set goals and expectations, I participated in several corporate committees, and I came in early and left late. I made sure the partner knew about all my extracurricular activities, like volunteering and community involvement, in hopes of separating myself from the pack. So I asked him, "In your opinion, what can I continue to do to keep getting excellent performance reviews?"

He looked at me and sighed as he said, "Jeff, it's great that you are participating in committees, focus groups, and extra activities, but my advice to you regarding continuous top-performance reviews is to *just perform*. Performing is really all that matters. I do care about the other stuff; however, if you're not performing, then who cares?" This conversation with the partner had a lasting impact on the way I would approach performance related activities from that point. I realized that I needed to consistently develop a habit, mindset, and strategy for maximizing my performance in my daily life.

In my pursuit to develop the most comprehensive, consistent, and nearly foolproof performance formula, I created this pillar based performance system through extensive study, research and diverse personal experiences. Through my findings, I learned that you can practically guarantee performance by building on these pillars.

This book is about pillars—eight pillars to be exact. But what exactly is a pillar, and how is it relevant to optimum performance? A pillar in architecture is an upright, tubular structure that is usually made of stone, brick, wood, metal, or some other strong and solid material. In most cases, it is relatively slender in proportion to its height, with either a round or square shape. Pillars are typically used to support different structures such as buildings, archways, and roads, or sometimes you find them just standing by themselves.

In some cases, pillars are used as monuments, similar to the Washington Monument in Washington DC. However, the pillars describe in this book represent pillars that stand together for greater productivity. Each pillar is needed to help productivity reach its peak, or optimum, level. When all the pillars work together and are strong independently, the overall group of pillars is even stronger, and then the chances for consistent, dependable, and reliable optimum performance increases.

CHAPTER 3

The Well-Rounded Beast: EPOP™

Pillar Philosophy

As I mentioned earlier, film director James Cameron created, in my humble opinion, the best movie ever made: *Avatar*. Although this movie—somehow—did not win Best Picture at the Oscars in 2010 (can you even remember what picture won?), it was light-years above its competitors. The movie *Avatar* is impressive, grand, beautiful, powerful, and visually stunning. If you haven't seen the movie by now, shame on you. Go rent it now, and watch it! We'll wait here until you get back...

James Cameron knows how to create movies that have leave strong and long-lasting impressions. Not only did *Avatar* have the most stunning visual effects of its time, it had a deep message about corporate greed and the importance of protecting and bonding with the environment. The movie also created a new language and a new culture. When you study the entire process of how the movie was created, developed, organized, marketed, and received, it makes a great case study for the Eight Pillars of Optimum Performance (EPOP™) philosophy. The making and then the release of the movie thoroughly covers the ideas behind EPOP™.

I could go on and on about this film; however, that's not the point. The point is to ask how a movie can outperform its competitors in most of the major categories and measuring sticks. It did this by adhering to the EPOP™ principles.

The Eight Pillars of Optimum Performance

(EPOP™) is a winning performance-enhancement system that consists of eight corresponding and balanced performance principles designed to help you reach your maximum potential. These eight principles work together in harmony using a balanced approach to help you reach the most comprehensive, holistic, continuous, and consistent optimum performance in activities involving work, business, school, sport, and home.

EPOP™ is not just about performing well, it is about reaching your *full* optimum performance level in whatever you are trying to achieve. It is about using all the capabilities at your disposal to perform at your highest level. In order to achieve maximum and optimum performance, you must develop skills in a number of key areas, and then balance those skills to complete and finish the task at hand with sharp execution and authority.

The EPOP™ philosophy consists of eight independent performance principles or characteristics working together to develop an optimum-performance profile.

Eight Pillars of Optimum Performance (EPOP™)

1. **Preparation:** The first step in achieving optimum performance is to effectively and thoroughly *prepare* for the targeted activity. Preparation involves developing an end-to-end plan. The plan should identify the five *W*s: who, what, where, when, and why (and also how). In order to be adequately prepared, the overall strategy, vision, goals, objectives, and actions need to be identified, understood, and executed. The essence of this Preparation Pillar is to plan, organize, manage time, research, set expectations, and be mentally and physically ready.

2. **Skill:** This pillar focuses on identifying and understanding your current skill level and ability to perform the targeted activity. In order to perform optimally in any activity, you need some level of skill.

3. **Knowledge**: The Knowledge Pillar is designed to help you optimize your performance. Here, you can utilize techniques that will enable you to enhance performance. The primary focus of this pillar concentrates on how and when to seek more knowledge through education, instruction, training, coaching, and tutoring.

4. **Practice:** Practice and repetition are the keys to ensuring successful preparation and knowledge gathering so you can achieve optimal results. After you gain the appropriate knowledge, you need to practice if you plan to be an optimal performer.

5. **Communication**: The Communication Pillar binds all the others together. Getting clear, concise, and effective information in the most efficient and productive manner is paramount for you to succeed in achieving your goal of performing at the highest level.

6. **Desire**: Of all the EPOP™ pillars, the Desire Pillar is the differentiator. You can prepare all you want, you can get all the proper training and education, and you can practice what you've learned—however, if you don't have the desire to push yourself to work hard and go the extra mile, you will not reach your optimum performance.

7. **Focus**: The aim of this pillar is to keep you on track with your goals. With so many distractions around us, staying focused can be a real challenge. Yet it will take focus for you to achieve optimum performance in anything. Being productive means being focused. One of the main reasons people struggle to perform in their academic, athletic, professional, and personal endeavors is simply a lack of focus.

8. **Execution:** In order to achieve optimum performance in whatever activity you choose, you need to execute the fundamental aspects of these eight pillars. Execution is about the actual *doing* of the activity. Whether you actually reach optimum performance depends on how well you execute. This pillar provides targeted instruction to get you in a finishing, get-it-done, and game-on execution mind-set.

Essentially, EPOP™ adheres to the philosophy of "two heads are better than one," except it is *"eight* heads are better than one." For example, a person can definitely perform using only one of the pillar principles (e.g., the Skill Pillar). However, performance will be more consistent, effective, frequent, predictable, and optimal utilizing some, or all, of the EPOP™ principles.

Take public speaking, for example. You might have a public speaker who has the ability to speak really well and to capture a crowd through a mesmerizing voice and unique command of the English language. This characteristic is the skill set or ability (Pillar Two). However, during the speech the speaker may not have all the proper facts (Pillar One), or the proper training (Pillar Three) that is needed to execute a clear, concise, and coherent speech. Also, the speaker may not have done the proper preparation and planning (Pillar One) in terms of the audience or the subject matter.

In addition, if the speaker loses focus or is distracted (Pillar Seven) or is all over the place in the speech with no organization, continuity, or flow (Pillar One), the chances for success are minimal. The speaker may also lack the knowledge to wrap up in a timely manner or finish with the wrong point (Pillar Eight). What you would have is a good speaker with a bad speech with a high probability of producing poor results.

However, by developing the other pillars, such as preparation and planning, the speaker would have enough foresight to organize the speech with the proper flow. With proper preparation and knowledge, the speaker could dig deeper into the subject matter and find out what the audience wanted to hear. In addition, with EPOP™, the speaker would get the proper training, quick supplemental instruction or coaching, or proper knowledge on how to speak in certain environments if there were any flaws in ability. The speaker would incorporate practice and repetition (Pillar Four) until the speech became almost second nature in order to deliver the speech in a natural manner. Finally, by incorporating EPOP™, the speaker would learn to focus, limit distractions, and hone in on the point.

Following these EPOP™ principles will lead to an optimum performance rather than one by someone who can speak fairly well. This is, in essence, what the EPOP™ pillar strategy is all about. It is about awakening and using your strengths and abilities by refining several areas of your character. It helps you realize some of the strengths you already know, and it helps you to discover where you need to get better. Then you are able to work on those other areas of weakness until you become a more balanced, more effective performer in whatever field you're trying to excel in.

Each Pillar Adds Strength

The EPOP™ philosophy is based on the principle that more is better. You increase your chances of higher performance and a more successful outcome with every pillar you use. As you increase your pillar usage from one pillar to two pillars to three, all the way up to eight, you improve your chances of delivering an optimum performance.

CHAPTER 4

How Does EPOP™ Work?

magine you just completed an activity where you didn't do as well as you expected. Or imagine you have an upcoming activity that you want to do your absolute best in. That's where EPOP™ comes in. The approach was created to help you position yourself to do the optimum best in any activity you try.

For example, let's say you have an important paper on China you need to write and deliver (whether for school or business). Hopefully, you will deliver the best work you can do. After your first attempt at writing the paper is complete and possibly ready to be delivered to your teacher or boss, try rating it from one to ten (with ten being the optimum). What rating would you give your paper?

The philosophy behind EPOP™ is that any rating under eight needs to be improved. Examine anything that is an eight or nine to see if getting to ten is possible. If not, then the eight or nine will be acceptable.

EPOP™ Profile Development and Identification

In order to work toward your goal of achieving optimum performance and success, you must first develop your EPOP™ profile and assessment by completing a Pillar Evaluation, which entails identifying the number of applicable pillars, pillar strengths, and what to do to get to optimum pillar strength for the specific tasks at hand. This evaluation is accomplished by completing an EPOP™-PA (Eight Pillars of Optimum Performance Profile and Assessment) form. Then you can determine your overall position to help you identify key areas of improvement for each pillar where you need to enhance your performance level.

By identifying these pillar gaps, you will be able to put strategies in place to improve the level of performance of the impacted pillar. Once you have enhanced each pillar with gaps to its optimum level, and no more performance enhancements can be recognized, you have achieved optimum performance for the first seven pillars, and you are ready to execute Pillar Eight.

EPOP™ Rating System from One to Ten:

Rating	Rating Description	Performance Expectations
10	Excellent	Excellent pillar execution expected: great shape; don't change a thing; no room for improvement
8–9	Good	Good pillar execution expected: good shape; slight room for improvement
5–7	Average	Fair to average pillar execution expected: improvement in some areas recommended
3–4	Below Average	Below average pillar execution expected: performance overhaul recommended
1–2	Poor	Poor pillar and EPOP™ execution expected: critical improvement needed; lots of work needed in this pillar

How Would You Rate the Finished Product?

Would you give your paper a seven, a three, or even a ten? How did you come up with that rating? What criteria did you use? Did you rate your paper based on the way it looked, or did you rate it based on the way it read? Was the rating based on how much time you spent on it, or if it had a lot of buzzwords?

Let's say you gave it a seven:

- Why a seven?
- What do you need to do to get it to an eight, nine, or ten?
- What are the gaps?
- What more do you need to do to improve?
- Is this the best you can do?

As you can see, you can always "guesstimate," speculate on, or presume what the results can be without a structured approach to getting results. However, you can use a more structured, organized, and results-oriented approach to assess the rating of your chosen activity (in this example, the paper on China).

That approach is to use the EPOP™ formula, which breaks your activity into eight separate, but related, components called pillars. Each pillar represents an area that you should assess and work toward enhancing until optimum performance is reached.

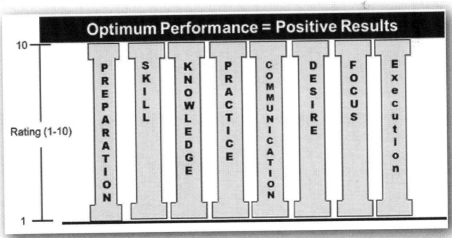

Copyright © 2015 Ainiare Enterprises

In the EPOP™ approach, each pillar has a maximum strength or rating of ten. However, realistically, it is more feasible to set goals of reaching eight in each pillar, and then work your way up to a ten, if possible.

Using the simple EPOP Formula®, you can deductively and structurally assess your anticipated results for the activity.

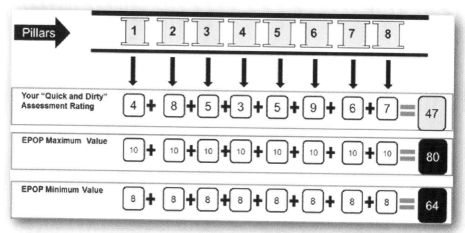

Copyright © 2015 Ainiare Enterprises

Here, the cumulative total of the quick-and-dirty rating is forty-seven, whereas the maximum EPOP™ value is equal to eighty (8 pillars x 10 rating), and the minimum EPOP™ value is sixty-four (8 pillars x 8 rating). Thus, there is some room to improve the China paper.

An additional way to quickly identify your proximity to the target goal is by using the EPOP™ Index. This is a simple indicator from one to ten. In order to have a favorable EPOP™ Index that would help render consistent and positive results in the activity, the Index should be at an eight or higher. If it is lower, then you should continually improve the activity.

The EPOP™ Index is calculated by dividing the "Total Assessment Value" by the numbers of pillars (eight) like so:

EPOP™ Index = Total Assessment Value / 8

Here are sample calculations using the China paper example:

- Total Assessment Value = 47

- EPOP™ Index [China paper] = 47 / 8 = 5.88
- Since 5.88 is well short of 8+, improvement activities are in order

Now go back to your quick-and-dirty assessment, and evaluate areas where you can enhance your performance results and improve your EPOP™ Index. First, identify each pillar with a value of less than eight:

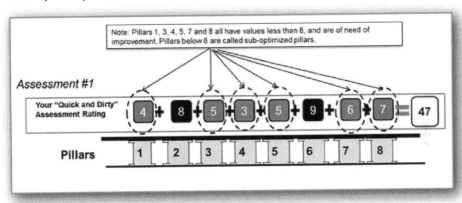

After identifying the suboptimized pillars, start the process to optimize each one using the POP (Pillar-Optimization Process) starting with Pillar One and proceeding through Pillar Eight (i.e., left to right).

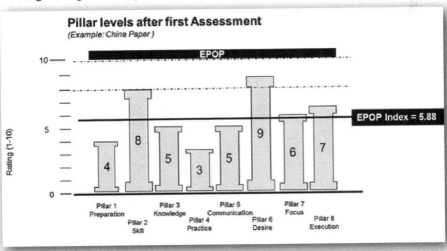

This chart provides a visual representation of how each pillar rates against the maximum EPOP™ Index (ten) and the Minimum EPOP™ Index (eight). For example, the above assessment of the China paper is a 5.88 EPOP™ Index. Several suboptimized pillars are below the minimum EPOP Index, causing the overall China paper EPOP™ Index to be lower than the minimum EPOP™ Index.

To improve the suboptimized pillars, you would go through the Pillar-Optimization Process (POP) for each pillar. The POP process can take anywhere from hours to months depending on the complexity of the activity and the extent of improvement needed. Once you have implemented the improvements, you'll need to reassess your current EPOP™ status to determine the revised EPOP™ Index.

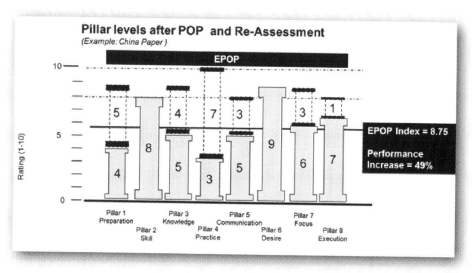

Copyright © 2015 Ainiare Enterprises

In the China paper example above, significant improvement was made in all the original suboptimized pillars.

Pillar Improvement Analysis Table
(Example: China Paper)

	Pillars									
	1	2	3	4	5	6	7	8	Total EPOP™ Value	EPOP™ Index
Assessment #1 Pillar Rating	4	8	5	3	5	9	6	7	47	5.88
Improvement Increase from Assessment #1 to Assessment #2	5	0	4	7	3	0	3	1	--	--
Revised Assessment Rating	**9**	**8**	**9**	**10**	**8**	**9**	**9**	**8**	**70**	**8.75**
Improvement % Increase	125%	0%	80%	233%	60%	0%	50%	14%	49%	49%

After the POP, the EPOP™ Index improved by 49 percent from 5.88 to 8.75. Most of the pillars improved in performance, except for the two pillars that were already optimized. There were major jumps in Pillar One (Preparation) and Pillar Four (Practice). With an EPOP™ Index at 8.75, the China paper is within the optimized space (i.e., eight to ten). It is now your decision whether to further optimize the paper or complete the activity.

Using the EPOP™ to Get the Results You Want

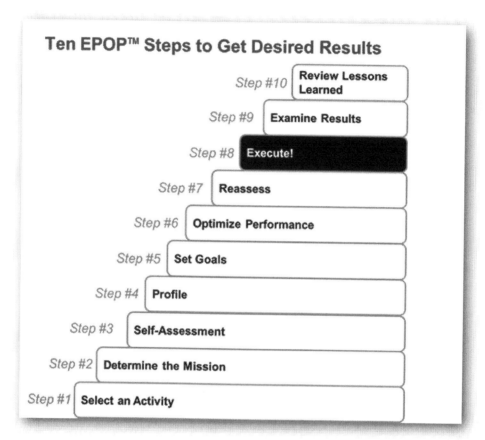

Copyright © 2015 Ainiare Enterprises

Step 1: Select an Activity

Select the activity or discipline you wish to perform. Although the possibilities are endless, here are some of the most common activities for which to apply the EPOP™ approach.

Work

- job interviews
- overall performance
- seeking promotion
- career change
- résumé development
- writing a paper
- enhancing computer skills
- presentations

Business

- presentations
- sales pitch
- bids or proposals
- speech
- management and leadership enhancement
- communication

Sports

- improving personal best (e.g., improving time to complete a 5K)
- golf performance
- overall better athletic performance
- basketball (shooting, dribbling, rebounding)
- baseball (pitching, hitting, fielding)
- football (tackling, blocking, catching, running)
- any sport

School

- SAT test and other standardized tests
- professional exams, such as PMP and LSAT
- better test scores
- writing a paper

- studying
- homework
- math
- writing
- presentations

Home

- gardening
- volunteering
- playing an instrument
- auditions
- learning a new language
- DIY projects

Step 2: Determine the Mission

Determine what you are trying to achieve at a high level with this activity. Here are some example mission statements for activities.

Work

- nail this job interview
- write a knockout paper that will thoroughly impress my boss and colleagues

Business

- put together a winning presentation
- win this bid or proposal

Sports

- improve my golf handicap by ten points in six months
- improve my personal-best 5K time by ten minutes in the next race

School
- optimize my SAT score
- increase my GPA up to optimum level

Home

- learn how to play X number of songs on my guitar independently
- learn to speak Chinese fluently in the next year

Step 3: Perform EPOP™ Self-Assessment

After determining what activity you want to increase your performance in, you then need to honestly and accurately assess your current EPOP™ progress in each pillar by completing one of the EPOP™ Assessment Tools. In the EPOP™ approach, there are three ways to get an assessment:

1. Quick-and-Dirty Assessment
2. Simple Form Assessment
3. Detailed Assessment

An assessment will provide a starting point and a calibration point of your current performance. After taking the initial assessment, you can determine what you need to improve, if necessary. The target EPOP™ Index is eight. If after any assessment the EPOP™ index is less than eight, then you should work on continuous improvement until your EPOP™ Index surpasses eight or you are satisfied that optimum level has been reached.

Quick-and-Dirty Executive-Level Assessment

The first assessment is the quick-and-dirty assessment (QAD), which you might use if you want quick, high-level answers without all the fuss about forms and applications.

This assessment is useful if you are familiar with the EPOP™ approach, and you don't really need to go through a detailed walk-through to get a sense of what needs to be improved. You can do the QAD assessment on a simple sheet of paper, napkin, or even the back of a receipt.

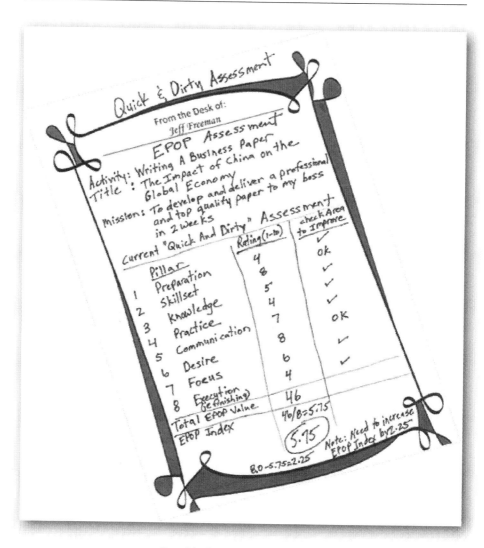

Write the activity name, activity title (if necessary), and the mission at the top of the page. On the left-hand side, make a list from one to eight, and label it with the corresponding pillar name (i.e., 1. Preparation or 8. Execution). Next, write out the headings: Pillar, Rating (1–10), and "Check Area to Improve."

To do the assessment, rate how ready you are right now to deliver the activity for each pillar. For example, for the Preparation Pillar (Pillar One), how prepared are you to complete the activity (i.e., have you set and met your goals and objectives, are you organized and have everything in order, is your strategy known and in place, and is your overall schedule and plan in place and ready to execute?)

Using your gut, rate where you are within that pillar from one to ten (with ten being excellent). Put that rating next to the pillar name to the right and under the rating heading. Rate each pillar from Preparation to Execution. Once completed, total your ratings, and place the sum next to the field marked "Total." Then find the EPOP™ Index by dividing the total by eight, and write that number under the EPOP™ Total Value. Finally, circle the EPOP™ Index.

Now go to the column marked "Check Area to Improve." For each pillar rating that is less than eight, mark the field with a check mark. Mark each pillar rating that is eight or above with "OK." You will implement improvement plans for pillars marked with a check. From the check marked pillars, start improving the pillars with the lowest rating first.

Once you've made all the improvements you think are possible, perform the assessment again until the EPOP™ Index is above eight.

Simple Form Assessment: EPOP™ EZ Form (www.ainiare.com)
The EPOP™ EZ Form is the next level of assessment detail after the QAD Assessment. It is designed to provide you with more structure and guidance. In addition to helping calculate the EPOP™ Index, the EZ Form enables you to identify the problems, issues, and gaps in each sub-performing pillar. Also, it allows an initial space for you to begin mapping out a skeleton plan for how to address and fix the issues and gaps for each of those pillars.

After thoroughly completing the form, you should use this EZ Form as a guide for improving your performance for the chosen activity.

Detailed Assessment: EPOP™ Profile Assessment (www.ainiare.com)
After determining what activity you want to increase performance in, your next step is to honestly assess your current EPOP™ progress in each pillar by completing the EPOP™ Profile Assessment.

- In order to work toward your goal of achieving optimum performance and success, you must first develop your EPOP™ Profile Assessment by completing a Pillar Evaluation, which entails identifying the number of pillars you need to work on, what each pillar's current strength is, and what to do to get to optimum pillar strength for the specific tasks.

- You accomplish this evaluation by completing an EPOP™-PA Form.
- Once you finish the EPOP™-PA, you will be able to determine your overall EPOP™ position.
- You will also identify key areas of improvement for each pillar where your performance level needs enhancement.
- By identifying these pillar gaps, you can put strategies in place to improve the level of performance of the impacted pillar.
- Once you've enhanced each pillar with gaps to its optimum level, and no more performance enhancements can be recognized, you have achieved optimum performance for the first seven pillars, and you are ready to execute Pillar Eight.

Step 4: Profile—Evaluate Your EPOP™ Self-Assessment

Analyze and examine pillars that have an EPOP™ index below eight. After assessing each pillar, evaluate each suboptimized pillar to determine if improvement is possible.

- Identify each suboptimized pillar (i.e., any pillar with a rating below eight).
- Evaluate in order, starting with Pillar One and ending with Pillar Eight.
- Evaluate the gaps, challenges, and/or issues that prevent this pillar from becoming optimized.
- Examine each gap, and indicate a fix to the issue, if possible. If not, indicate why not.
- Indicate the expected pillar rating after you implement improvements.

Step 5: Set EPOP™ Goals

If possible, set numerical optimum performance targets or goals for each pillar (both suboptimal and optimal). Identify when you want to achieve these milestones (time goals). Set up a "mini" project plan with a list of tasks to complete, the dates you want to complete these milestones, and who will be responsible for carrying out the tasks. After the goals and targets have been set, it's time to work on improving the suboptimal pillars.

Step 6: Optimize EPOP™ Performance

In this step, evaluate each suboptimized pillar to engage and work on enhancing and optimizing the EPOP™ performance. First, read through the relevant pillar section in the book, and apply, and implement any relevant tips and suggestions. Next, look at the key reference links within the pillar, and apply them to your situation if possible. Do this for any pillar you want to improve, especially for the suboptimized pillars.

Note: This improvement implementation process can take anywhere from hours to months to implement and complete.

Step 7: Reassessment

When you think you've made the appropriate amount of progress to reach your target goals, do a reassessment. Perform a reassessment using the same method as the initial assessment by using one of the three assessment tools.

Step 8: Execute!

Actually engage the activity. If you have performed the reassessment and the EPOP™ Index is above eight, then you are ready for execution. In other words, you are ready to take the test, turn in the paper, present the speech, run the race, perform in the music recital, or play in the golf tournament.

Step 9: Examine Your Results

Review success-criteria metrics to determine if you achieved the desired results. Thoroughly examine the details of the activity section by section. Break the whole into parts, and examine each area. For example, if your target activity was to reduce your golf score from ninety to eighty, first look at your score. Did you hit your target? Whether you did or not, break down the score at each hole. How well did you drive the ball? How many times did you hit the fairway? How many greens in regulation did you have? How many putts did you have once you made it to the green? As you break down the sections, you may begin to discover areas of deficiency that, if corrected, can improve your score even more. This results breakdown method can be implemented for any and all activities, not just those that are sports related.

Step 10: Review Lessons Learned (Optional)

Win or lose, review how you can improve next time. Document what you learned that could help you in future challenges. Maybe you realized that you were a better researcher than you thought. Perhaps distractions were a major problem. Maybe you procrastinated much more than you thought. Write down any and all lessons or items you learned about yourself and the activity.

CHAPTER 5

Don't Get Caught
Slippin': Be Prepared

Pillar One: Preparation

This first Preparation Pillar is essential to ultimate performance. Lack of preparation is the single most common cause of people achieving less-than-optimum success in their particular ventures. The essence of preparation is to try to foresee upcoming events and activities, and have a prepared response for them. Optimum performance starts with a vision or ultimate target of what you hope to achieve. The more you can visualize the optimum performance, the closer you can get to achieving it. Once you have a clear vision of success in your mind, you need to determine how to prepare in order to achieve success.

For example, if you have your eye on changing your job or career, you need to find out the requirements for the new job (i.e., skill set, education, experience, and location), and then seek and secure the elements required. Preparation will not guarantee success, but it will put you a lot closer to it. Most importantly, the preparation you put into getting ready for the right opportunity will increase the likelihood of running into it. Preparation allows you to develop a response, options, or actions to combat the problem or challenge when it occurs.

Preparation does not always lead to success; in fact, the other pillars may have more influence on the outcome than preparation does. However, preparation puts you in a better position to succeed. For example, before the 2014 Super Bowl, Peyton Manning expressed that the key to victory for the Denver Broncos was to be extremely prepared for the Seattle Seahawks. So Manning prepared diligently. He looked at all the available film of his opponents; he studied their formations, their tendencies, their weaknesses and strengths. He even talked to other opponents who had some success against the Seahawks to find out how they achieved that success. Based on his research and due diligence, he and his coach put together an effective and thorough game plan. However, the Seahawks whipped the Broncos.

Preparation is one of the most important pillars, as some of the other pillars (Knowledge, Practice, and Communication) are dependent on it. Preparation helps you understand what you need to do in order to reach those optimum performance levels you so desire.

Keys to Successful Preparation

1. Create a preparation checklist.
2. Understand thoroughly what you are trying to accomplish.
3. Plan your activity.
4. Get organized.
5. Manage your time wisely.
6. Research the subject and your competitors.

1. Create a Preparation Checklist

A checklist is a good place to start the preparation process. On a clean sheet of paper, list key preparation items and milestones. These milestones should cover who, what, where, when, and how preparation tasks.

Check off key preparation activities as you progress through the process.

Since activities are different and can have unique preparation tasks, a checklist can have various entries. In general, checklist should include the following tasks:

- Identify the activity
- Target activity execution date, time, duration
- Determine activity costs, such as registration fees
- Identify your activity performance gaps and needs
- Identify a strategy to resolve and mitigate gaps
- Determine preparation activities

- Outline practice schedule
- List materials and costs needed to prepare:
  - Book(s)
  - Preparation class(es)
  - Online preparation tests
- Determine activity success criteria
- Understand where activity will take place

2. Thoroughly Understand What You Are Trying to Accomplish

Here are some tools you can use to pinpoint and define your specific goals:

- mission statement
- objectives and goal setting
- SWOT analysis
- understanding of requirements
- understanding of success criteria
- schedule, timelines, and milestones
- knowledge of your competition

The Mission Statement

During the planning phase, you need to have some overall purpose or result that the plan will achieve in mind (consciously or unconsciously). For example, during strategic planning, it's critical to reference the mission or overall purpose of the organization.

The mission statement is a broad, general statement that states what you are trying to achieve in this activity. By definition, a "mission" is a large, long-standing feat or accomplishment. There may be strategies, goals, objectives, actions, schemes, and executions all used to achieve the mission, but the mission is the biggest and most important thing to be accomplished.

The mission statement clearly states the purpose of the activity, and it usually does not change. For example, your activity may be to give a keynote speech to graduating business students regarding the impact of the rise of India and China in the global marketplace. Therefore, your mission would be, "To present a rousing, informative, motivating speech that will entertain and educate America's future business leaders on the global financial impact of the Chinese and Indian markets." That basically explains what you want to accomplish as an end result.

Objectives and Goal Setting (What Are You Actually Trying to Achieve?)

Within EPOP™, goals and objectives have similar characteristics. There can be a number of objectives and goals that you need to accomplish in order to achieve a mission, but there is usually only *one* mission. "Goals" are statements that describe what you wish to accomplish. The goal should relate to the mission and purpose of your activity.

Goals are powerful because without them people forget or don't know what they are trying to achieve. Not having goals can blind you from some of your dreams. For instance, at first glance you may think that an item you want to purchase or a trip you want to take is too expensive or unreachable, so you get discouraged and don't bother trying to reach for it. However, if you set a realistic goal to achieve what you want, the chances of achieving it increase significantly.

For example, when we got married, my wife and I set a goal to travel somewhere every year regardless of our situation. It didn't matter if the venture was international or domestic, we would go somewhere. So we included travel in our annual budget planning. As part of our financial strategy from year to year, along with planning our savings and retirement finances we set aside six to fifteen thousand dollars for travel expenses. That's how important travel was to us.

If we didn't make travel a goal at the beginning of the year, and we had a lean year, then we wouldn't have the money in the budget. Our response in those years would be, "Oh well, this year we won't be able to travel anywhere," and, over time, it would get easier to not do what we wanted to do. However, in the twenty years that we have been together, my wife and I have traveled around the world, been on ten cruises, gone to Hawaii several times, and so on. I know colleagues and friends of mine who haven't gone on even one trip—basically because they didn't set a travel goal.

Each goal should have a number of objectives associated with it. Once you identify the objectives, it is important to develop a plan of action for each objective.

"Objectives" are descriptions of exactly what needs to be done in order to accomplish each goal. Objectives should be clear and specific statements of measurable tasks that you will accomplish as steps toward reaching your goals. Objectives set the plan of action for the activity, and they should be short term and have deadlines. Objectives are selected to be timely and indicative of progress toward goals.

For example, if your goal is to lose weight, your objective would be the target weight you are trying to lose in the designated period of time: for instance, "I want to lose twenty pounds in four weeks." The goal is simply to lose weight; however, the objectives are indicated by how much you want to lose and in what time frame.

For example, going back to the China and India speech, are you trying to raise money or funds for charity, increase membership in an organization, or make money from this activity? You need to determine what your goals are, and then you can establish objectives for each goal. After establishing objectives, you can then develop and execute the action plan.

Consider these goals, objectives, and action plans for the China and India speech example.

Goal	Objectives	Actions
To profit off the speech	To make $10,000 from this event	Secure a speaker fee and sell products
To get more speaking engagements invitations or opportunities to other events	• Get 5 or more referrals • Get 20 business cards	Network with the audience after the speech
To get the audience to buy a CD or recording of the speech	• To sell 50 CDs @ $15.99 (on-site) • To see an online increase of 15% for the next week following the speech	Setup a product selling table Mention website during the speech
To sell books	• To sell 50 CDs @ $15.99 (on-site) • To see an online increase of 15% for the next week following the speech	Setup a product selling table Mention website during the speech
To get the audience to go to a website	To see website traffic increase by 15% directly after the speech	Monitor traffic before and after speech

The SWOT Analysis (What Is the Assessment?)

"SWOT" is an acronym for the areas of assessment: strength, weaknesses, opportunities, and threats. When strategic planners conduct SWOT planning for big projects, they often assess the organization's strategic position. However, for the purpose of this book, you will produce a SWOT analysis for your activity. First you need to complete an EPOP™ Self-Assessment. In short, you need figure out who you are and exactly what are you trying to accomplish.

After the EPOP™ Self-Assessment, perform a SWOT for the target activity:

- identify your strengths (within EPOP™)
- identify your weaknesses
- identify your opportunities: for growth
- identify your threats

For instance, if a SWOT is done on the China and India speech, you would need to identify your strengths for developing and delivering the speech at a high EPOP™ performance level. Basically, you could identify the following traits from an EPOP™ perspective:

Strength Statements:

Statement	EPOP™ Pillar Category	EPOP™ Pillar Number
I am a natural and skilled public speaker	Skill	Pillar #2
I am in control when speaking in public	Skill	Pillar #2
I have a strong background in Chinese and Indian cultures	Knowledge	Pillar #3
I communicate well with others	Communication	Pillar #5
I am interested in and have a passion for the subject matter	Desire	Pillar #6

Weakness Statements:

Statement	EPOP™ Pillar Category	EPOP™ Pillar Number
I am not a good planner	Preparation	Pillar #1
I am not well-organized	Preparation	Pillar #1
I don't always manage my time appropriately	Preparation	Pillar #1
I don't have the best study and practice habits	Practice	Pillar #4
I don't know how to use e-mail, instant messaging, and PowerPoint	Communication	Pillar #5
I am not a strong typist	Skill	Pillar #2
I get distracted easily by web surfing and social networking	Focus	Pillar #7

Opportunity Statements:

Statement	EPOP™ Pillar Category	EPOP™ Pillar Number
Improve planning, organization, and time- management skills	Preparation	Pillar #1
Improve practice and study skills	Practice	Pillar #4
Learn basic contemporary communication skills	Communication	Pillar #5
Enroll in a typing class or hire someone to do the typing	Communication	Pillar #5
Develop techniques and methods to help limit distraction and threats	Focus	Pillar #7

Threat Statements:

Statement	EPOP™ Pillar Category	EPOP™ Pillar Number
Lack of time to do any of the work	Preparation	Pillar #1
Lack of funds to get to the venue to give the speech	Preparation	Pillar #1
Someone is doing the same subject-matter speech just before me	Preparation	Pillar #1

Do your analysis, and align your thoughts on what you need to work on, because that sets up the planning for everything else.

Understanding the Success Criteria

Success criteria are the specific, concrete, and measurable performance targets. They describe what success looks like when you reach your activity performance. You need to thoroughly understand what success means to you for each activity. A success criterion can be a certain metric you are trying to achieve. For example, when taking the SAT exam, your success criterion may be getting greater than 1900 on the exam.

Understanding Requirements

In order to reach the success criteria mentioned above, you need to understand the basic necessities, resources and prerequisites required to achieve them. In many situations, you cannot even reach your ultimate goals until you have satisfied the underlying activity requirements.

For example, if you want to be a lawyer, you can't just start telling everyone you're a lawyer. There are several requirements that need to be fulfilled before becoming an attorney (Findlaw.com 2014). To start, you first need a bachelor's degree. Then you need to take the LSAT exam, go to law school, and take the bar exam. And there are many more requirements. The point is that for whatever activity you choose, first understand, identify, and complete the requirements.

Schedule, Timeline, and Milestones
An important part of preparation is establishing a schedule to complete your activity. Within the schedule, you should set time lines to complete required tasks to ensure you are progressing toward your goal. Time lines are the dates you set to achieve each task.

In addition to time lines, you should also include milestones in your schedule. These are important dates or events you monitor throughout your activity until completion. Milestones help you keep track of key dates, key deadlines, expirations, and external dates.

Know Your Competition
If your activity involves competing against someone else, such as a sales pitch, interview, or sports, it is advantageous to learn about your competition as much as possible. As best you can, profile your competition by finding out the background, history, personnel, and tendencies. Also, try to understand strengths and weaknesses. Try to determine how the competition is a threat to your success, and how you may be able to exploit opportunities.

Of course, this book concentrates on how you can improve and become the best you can be; however, it never hurts to understand what you are competing against to get the upper hand.

3. Plan Your Activity
If you've ever coached youth sports, you know the serious need to plan. Although coaching is volunteer work and a community service, the parents of your youth athletes will tell you that you need to plan activities as if it were your job.

As a coach of many of my son's teams through the years, developing a plan and executing it are imperative to having a successful season in the parents' eyes. It is not always about the wins and losses to the parents; rather, success usually comes down to if the families had good experiences participating on your team. That good experience usually is determined by you appearing organized, control, and competent; properly communicating key information; and helping make the kids better athletes and people. These attributes are more successful when you have properly planned your season. When you're in charge of twenty-plus kids after school every day, you need a solid plan in place for organizing and utilizing their time efficiently and effectively, or you will be eaten alive by angry parents.

From the first parent introduction meeting to the final awards ceremony banquet, you have to carefully plan the practice schedule, games, pizza parties, fundraising activities, parent-involvement activities, and league meetings. And that's not even the coaching part. In addition, you have to plan your coaching staff, conditioning exercises, plays to run, and overall game planning. Without planning, I could have looked like a disorganized, incompetent, and out-of-control coach. Then the parents would have had second thoughts about putting their kids in my care.

The key component of preparation is planning. It is the first building block of the Preparation Pillar because it can help build a foundation for other performance components. "Planning" is basically the process of deciding what to do and how to do it. When and if things go wrong, the mishap can generally be traced back to poor planning or the failure to follow an existing plan. As the saying goes, "Failing to plan means you are planning to fail." This is a common cliché; however, at its core, the saying effectively highlights why planning is so important to optimum performance.

Napoleon Hill once said, "The successful leader must plan his work, and work his plan. A leader who moves by guesswork, without practical, definite plans, is comparable to a ship without a rudder. Sooner or later he will land on the rocks" (Hill 1937). A plan provides you with the ability to anticipate potential problems, and it helps to design a framework to avoid most possible negative outcomes while propelling you toward the desired results. Very simply put, planning sets the direction for activity, and then guides the activity along that direction. Planning can range from simple and basic to highly complex.

Common to these many complexities of planning are various phases of planning and guidelines for carrying those plans out as effectively as possible. Original plans do not always come out as intended. Put some anticipation into the plan, and plan for all possible scenarios. In other words, you need to have a Plan *A*, but you need to have a Plan *B*, a Plan *C*, and so on.

You need to anticipate any types of risks in your plan so you can find out how to mitigate them. For example, if you are giving a speech, and there is a risk that you will not be able to use your PowerPoint presentation on the large screen, then you need to mitigate that risk by having handouts available and by being so well versed in your speech so that you don't need to look at the presentation pieces or the presentation on the screen.

Many people take planning for granted, so they miss the opportunity to radically perfect their activity's final results. However, planning is the key ingredient in determining if your activity will be successful. Although there are different levels of planning—such as individual planning, group planning, corporate planning, and business planning—EPOP™ primarily focuses on individual planning in the areas of work, business, sports, school, and home. To plan out the target activity, EPOP™ uses the following model to help simplify the process:

Key EPOP™ Planning-Model Concepts

- identify the activity
- brainstorm
- develop an action plan
- implement
- work the plan
- examine planning results

This model is call the EPOP™ Planning Model, and it consists of the following process steps: First, *identify the activity* you are performing (i.e., a test, speech, or presentation). Next, take some time to *brainstorm* about what is involved in the target activity. Then, *develop an action plan* to guide you through the planning process by defining the overall mission, goals, and objectives of the activity. Once the plan is developed, you need to act on the tasks within the plan, and *implement* those actions. As you are implementing the plan, you need to continue to *work the plan* by monitoring and managing the plan's progression. Finally, once the activity has been executed, you need to *examine planning results* to determine if the goals and objectives have been satisfied.

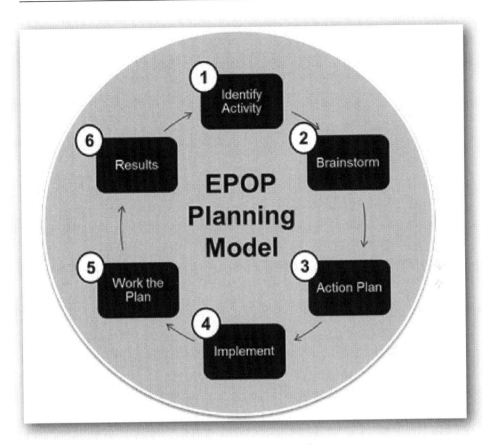

Copyright © 2015 Ainiare Enterprises

4. Get Organized

My teenage son is a star athlete and a great scholar (so I would like to think). He is also a typical teenage student with a messy work and study environment. He usually has papers everywhere, with books stacked on the desk in random order, some opened and some not. Snack remnants such as potato-chip bags, candy wrappers, and soda and juice cans are strewn everywhere, leftover from late-night and long-day study sessions.

One day when he was working on a school project, my son was looking for a simple glue stick. Yes, a glue stick. As always, when he needed supplies, he went to the supply cabinet, where we store all the paper, pencils, paper clips, staples, and glue sticks. However, to his surprise, when he checked the cabinet, there were no glue sticks. So he texted his mom to ask where she thought more would be. She had him search his room, his work space, the supply cabinet again, our office—basically all the rooms in the house. Still, he couldn't locate the elusive glue sticks.

Since glue sticks are relatively cheap, my wife bought some more—in fact, she bought the jumbo pack of ten. In addition, she bought more pencils, pens, and other supplies, as she thought this was a sign that stationery supplies may be low.

When she got home, she went into our son's work/study area to give him the supplies. But when she the messy space, she told him to clean it up and put things in their proper places. Like most teenagers, he disputed that his way of organized chaos was comfortable to him, as he had his own unique system that his parents just didn't understand. Of course, his mom had none of it and made him clean it up.

After an hour or so, he started to discover pencils, pens, and important papers that had been hiding under the so-called "organized mess." Then, as he finally reached the desk, something popped out and fell on the floor. Not only was it a glue stick, but a fresh, unopened jumbo pack of ten, along with new packages of pencils and pens from the last trip to the stationery store.

So if my son's work environment had been clean and organized, where everything could be seen and was easily assessable and searchable, he would not have needed to waste time searching around the house. In addition, his mother wouldn't have needlessly spent her time and more money. That's the power of organization. This experience provided a lesson to my son about how valuable it is to keep all aspects of your life organized and in order.

According to Wikipedia, "Organizing is the act of rearranging elements following one or more rules." OK, so what does that mean, exactly? Wiki goes on to say, "Anything is commonly considered organized when it looks like everything has a correct order or placement. But it's only ultimately organized if any element has no difference on time taken to find it. In that sense, organizing can also be defined as 'to place different objects in logical arrangement for better searching'" (Wikipedia 2014).

Organizing is a key component in the Preparation Pillar. If you're not organized, you will not be adequately prepared. It's that simple. One of my key strengths is my ability to organize. And when I mention organizing, I'm not talking about lining up all the cups correctly in the cupboard, or lining up twenty white shirts and twenty blue ties and suits—no, not that type of organization. I'm referring to the ability to organize my projects, tasks, and activities in a clear and structured manner.

When you learn to organize and put things in their proper places, you're able to communicate more effectively and think a more clearly because things are laid out properly. You can produce at a more consistent and quicker pace than you could if you were not organized.

To assist me in staying organized and more productive at the office, I use the EPOP™ DRAFT organizing method. DRAFT: (Discard, Refer, Act, File, Table).

Discard

If paper items, such as, documents, reports, magazines, coupons, etc. will never be retrieved again, discard it. Saving unnecessary paper, clutters your files, your office, and your desk. Ask yourself whether another copy of a document you are saving is easily available if you need it. If the answer is yes, toss yours.

If you spend time searching through piles of papers on your desk or in your office looking for a specific document, search no more. As you are looking for that specific document, do you find yourself stopping and reading other documents in the pile again, over and over? The issue with this is that you are not only wasting time looking for one document, but you are wasting more time rereading other papers along the way.

All this wasted time can be turned into productive time. Find the secret to a clean, clear desk, and how to keep it that way. It's a great stress reliever. For helpful tips on reducing clutter, read Reduce Stress, Increase Productivity, and Enjoy Your Clutter-Free Life, by Michelle Stewart or Declutter Your Life: Quick and Easy Tips by Jenny Davis.

Refer

If someone else can do the paper work for you or if someone else needs it, pass it on, or give it up.

Act

Act on it now. Don't procrastinate. Do routine paper work immediately.

File

Don't let it sit there. With a proper filing system, important documents can be filed–and found—in a snap. There are primarily two types of filing systems: (1) Paperless and (2) Paper

A paperless filing system is a work environment in which the use of paper is eliminated or greatly condensed. This is accomplished by transforming documents and other papers into digital form. Going paperless can increase productivity, reduce cost, maximize office space, provide additional security, and allow for easier document and information sharing. To find out more about using a paperless filing system to organize your life read How to Go Paperless at Home – 11 Tips and Solutions (Levin, 2013).

If you haven't yet converted to a paperless filing system for handling documents, you can still easily manage a system to keep track of all you records. Traditional office have paper-based filing systems, which may include filing cabinets, folders, shelves, boxes, crates, bags, and drawing cabinets. Simple adjustments such as, purchasing a file cabinet, hanging folders, creating labels, organizing your documents and files, and discarding unneeded documents can save you plenty of time and frustration while increasing your productivity. To find out more about filing system and productivity, please read, Getting Things Done: The Art of Stress-Free Productivity by David Allen.

Table

Files or documents that you don't use on a regular basis, but you must keep for legal, historical, or financial reasons (such as taxes) need to be archived. If you need it at some time in the near future, other than today you can table the document by placing it in archival system for easy, quick access. Archiving is the storage or preservation of information. To find out more about effective document and file storage and archiving please read, Creating an Effective File System by Catherine Murphy and Susan Hale.

5. Manage Time Wisely

On my first business trip to London, being a car-hungry Southern California native, I was impressed with the effective and efficient use of mass transit. One can get around London easily via taxi, light-rail, train system, and, of course, the personal cars that drive on the wrong side of the street with passengers at the steering wheel.

The UK light-rail system, called the London Underground (also known as "the Tube"), is a rapid-transit system that the majority of Londoners use every day to move about town. Throughout my trip, I felt I could get anywhere in the city in the Tube, and I always made it to my destinations with plenty of time to spare. I could have taken taxis; however, they were more expensive and taxi drivers were kind of cranky and uninterested in short routes. I got so used to the efficiency of the Tube that I lost my need to effectively manage my time.

So when it was time for me to leave for the airport, I didn't use proper time management. When leaving for Heathrow Airport from my hotel, because of my newly found experience with London mass transit, I carelessly estimated it would take about an hour via the Tube or an hour and a half by taxi (due to traffic). Since I didn't want to haul my luggage around, I chose the taxi and left three hours before my flight. Plenty of time—so I thought.

As I rode through the city, I was awed by the beauty and history of this great city. I remember saying to myself, "I'm in London, really in London." No one in my immediate circle had been anywhere near London, and there I was, a kid from Inglewood, riding through one of the most historical, stunning, important cities in the world. As I admired my ride through the city, I didn't pay attention to the time. When we finally arrived at Heathrow, we arrived in two hours instead of my projected hour and a half due to the traffic.

Now I had only one hour to catch my flight—still enough time if I hurried. I ran through that airport like that famous football player called "the Juice." Believe it or not, I made it through Heathrow in about fifteen or twenty minutes. I ran toward the gate thinking, *I can do this; I can do this.* I couldn't believe it: I was about to luck out and catch an international flight back home without any real time management or planning.

I finally reached the gate, huffing and puffing. As I handed the gate attendant my ticket, she looked at it and said, "Sorry, due to security reasons all international flights must check in at least an hour before the flight time. You cannot get on this flight."

"But there's still forty minutes left. I can make it to the plane in ten!" I was furious. "I need to get back to the United States, and the plane hasn't left yet. Can you please make an exception?"

"No, you must catch the next flight, which is in only six hours," she said. "Perhaps you should have managed your time a little better, and then you may have been able to catch the flight on time."

I couldn't believe it. If I would have managed my time wisely and not tried to cut it so close, I would have saved six hours. My lesson: for each activity for which

I must meet a timeline, I need to make sure to leave plenty of time to make it, and I need to know all the timeline rules to factor into my time-management plans.

Time management is a major function in the Preparation Pillar, as in order to be successful you need to effectively navigate your life based on time lines and schedules. Time management is about controlling the use of your most valuable (and undervalued) resource. It's important because of the limitations that exist in everyday life. For example, there are only twenty-four hours in each day, and much of that time is consumed by activities we can't control, such as sleep (eight to ten hours), eating (one to two hours), commuting (zero to four hours), and employment (eight to ten hours). These activities can take up from seventeen to twenty-two hours a day, leaving you with two to seven hours for yourself and your family. How you manage those hours will determine your success.

A lack of time management is demonstrated by the phrase "running around like a chicken with its head cut off"—constantly being late or close to late for appointments and meetings, consistent late nights at the office, overlapping meetings, last-minute rushes to meet deadlines, meetings that are double-booked, unproductive days, and too many firefights on a daily basis. This sort of environment leads to unwarranted stress and degradation of performance that will impact your ability to reach your optimum capacity.

6. Research the Subject and Competitors (Do Your Due Diligence)

Within the EPOP™ system, research is the differentiator in the planning process. If done correctly, it will give you the edge you need to succeed. It is the ingredient that separates the top tier from the pack, the elite from the ordinary, the great from the good, the cream from the crop, and success from failure. You might ask, if research is so special and valuable, why doesn't everyone do it? The answer to this is simple: "People are *lazy!*" OK, not everyone, of course. However, in order to be an effective researcher, you need to dedicate time and extra work where sometimes the benefit is not truly known.

I Didn't Want to Do It!

I didn't want to do it! My boss at the time said, "You need to embrace this. You are an officer at this company, and if you can't do this, then perhaps we need to find someone else who can." The activity I originally wanted no part of was traveling to India on business to help in the preparations to transfer several staff positions from the United States and Europe to India.

I resisted traveling to India for a couple of reasons: (1) I didn't feel it was right or made good business sense to move these US and European jobs to a developing country, and (2) I had serious reservations, misguided perceptions, and a negative bias against India as a country. I was truly ignorant about the essence of the country other than what had been communicated in the news, on TV, and through the few Indian people I had observed in the United States.

But since this became a mandatory endeavor, I decided to embrace the opportunity and make the best of this situation. From that point, I was determined to learn more about India and its people, culture, economics, and politics. And the best way to come up to speed would be through research.

My first stop was to explore the various travel books and maps available from AAA, such as Frommer's and Fodor's. Next, I looked for books from online bookstores such as Amazon.com, BarnesandNoble.com, and Borders.com, as these virtual stores are always a great source of information. In many cases, you can narrow your search down to the specific details, and then you can purchase new and used books for affordable prices, sometimes under a buck.

Of course, while I was researching books online, I was simultaneously doing plenty of research on the web. I utilized the bountiful selection of search engines available: namely, Google, Yahoo, and Bing. Of course, there are hundreds of other search engines to choose from, but these three usually provide me with all the relevant information I need.

Finally, the most important research I did was to talk to coworkers who had recently taken similar trips to India. Fortunately, they provided valuable information that I couldn't find in a travel book, in the library, or even on the web: information such as which hotel worked best for the targeted work location, the need to have a driver and not drive yourself around, what areas to avoid, what shots are needed before the trip, what not to drink, and how to avoid getting sick, to name just a few.

Due to all of my research, I got a better profile of what I needed to understand about the country. What I found was that I didn't know about the country at all. I came to realize that much of what I had thought prior to my research was false information. What I ultimately discovered was that when armed with the appropriate information, I was not only ready to go to India, but I was excited and thrilled at the unique opportunity. As it turned out, that trip was one the most important and impactful journeys I've taken in my life, and I relish the thought of returning one day. At first I didn't want to do it, but after research and due diligence I was happy to go, and today I'm grateful and glad that I did.

CHAPTER 6

Either You Got It,
or You Don't

Pillar Two: Skill

American Idol is one of my favorite TV shows. It's a reality TV singing competition. The concept is to find a new solo recording artist, where the winner is determined by the TV viewers. However, before a winner is chosen, the contestants go through a long process that starts with the audition. In the early part of the selection process, the show travels to different cities where thousands of people come from all over to take advantage of the opportunity.

During these traveling auditions, the show uses three or four celebrity judges to make a quick (thirty- to sixty-second) assessment of each contestant's ability to sing. (I'm sure there is a filtering process before the contestant reaches the judges; however, that process is never revealed on the show.) So the judges decide on the spot whether or not a contestant moves on to the next round (which usually involves a trip to Hollywood). In order to have a chance of moving on, the contestants must be able to do one thing: sing. They must be able to wow the judges with their singing abilities and voices. At this point, the judges are only looking for someone to pump out some sweet melody. In short, they are looking for skill and raw talent.

At this point, it doesn't matter to the judges if contestants have been preparing (Pillar One) for this moment all their lives. It's all about the skill. It doesn't matter if the contestants have been professionally trained and learned music at one of the best musical schools in the country (Pillar Three), but only if they can *sing*. In fact, it is irrelevant whether the competitors can recite all the lyrics to Lady Gaga's songs or knows the names of all the number-one hits in the past ten years (Pillar Three). The judges don't care if the participants have practiced twenty-four hours a day, seven days a week for the past two weeks (Pillar Four), or that they say all the right things and have perfect smiles (Pillar Five), or that they have been dreaming of this moment and have the desire and passion to go all the way (Pillar Six). At this point, the contestants simply need to be able to blow the judges' minds with raw talent.

You get the point. In order to optimally succeed in any endeavor, you at least have to have the basic ability and skills to compete. Once you have those basic skills, you can use the other pillars, along with your skill set, to reach for optimum performance. For example, a bus driver cannot operate the bus without knowing how to drive. A surgeon who faints at the sight of blood will not be an effective and long-lasting surgeon. And a salesperson who is afraid to talk to people won't make many sales.

Understanding what skills you bring to the table of your chosen activity is the first step in determining how great you can actually be. Assessing your skills and determining your mental and physical abilities, competence, skill level, and whatever gifts or talents you have will help you decide what you need to do to become an optimum performer. It may be that, after an honest assessment, you may not be able to bring your skill-proficiency level up in time to accomplish whatever you are trying to do.

For example, imagine you were slightly overweight and had never run, jogged, or even walked a mile before. What if you suddenly decided that you wanted to run a marathon in under four hours in the next week? It's a fair bet that you would have neither the ability nor skill, physically or mentally, to accomplish this feat in that time frame. However, if you set your sights on accomplishing this feat in a year, or even in six months, with proper training (Pillar Three) and preparation (Pillar One), your skill proficiency should vastly improve.

The EPOP™ Skill-Proficiency Model (ESPM)

In the EPOP™ system, improving your overall skills is dependent on four corresponding but separate components:

1. ability
2. competence

3. skill
4. talent

This process is known as the EPOP™ Skill-Proficiency Model (ESPM)—*not* ESPN.

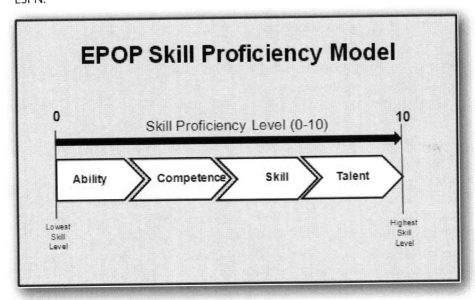

With ESPM, the goal is to determine the Skill-Proficiency Level (SPL) as shown in the diagram above. The SPL of your targeted activity can be determined by using a range of zero to ten, with zero being no skill level to ten being highest, or optimum, skill level. Your SPL increases as you increase the four components that make up the SPL (ability, competence, skill, and talent).

Ability

The first component of SPL is "ability," as one must be able to do the activity at its most basic and elementary level if there is any hope of optimal performance. Ability is the quality or state of being able to power, or even having the power to do so, whether physically, mentally, intellectually, morally, ethically, or legally. Being able means having the necessary means, skills, know-how, and/or authority to do something (e.g., to be able to swim, sing, and so on). In addition, ability means having the inherent physical or mental ability or capacity (for instance, human beings are able to walk on two feet) to perform the task.

Let's look at a simple example that explains how ability impacts the SPL. Imagine that a secretary is asked to type a document for the boss. In terms of ability, the secretary needs a couple of things to be able to even start. For example, the secretary must have a computer, must be able to know how to use a computer, must be able to touch the keys, must be able to see the keys, must be able to read, must have enough time, and so on. These (and more) are all requirements of a secretary having the ability to do the job.

Competence

Once you've determined that you are able to do the activity, you then need to determine how competent you are in doing the task. "Competence" is defined as the quality of being adequately or well qualified physically and intellectually. Within EPOP™, the difference between ability and competence is that with *ability* you have all the necessary requirements to be able to do the task, and most of the barriers or obstacles have been alleviated. However, it doesn't mean that you are qualified or ready to do the task or job. With competence, you have met the minimum qualifications to competently do the activity.

Competence is the next level of the skill proficiency that you want to reach in order to get closer to realizing your optimum best. When you are competent, you are secure in knowing you can do at least an average or adequate job to get by.

Take the typist example again. A competent typist has the ability to do the job and the minimum qualifications to accomplish the task. For example if the average professional can type at speeds of fifty to eighty words per minute (WPM). Therefore, a competent typist would be expected to type at least a minimum of 50 WPM. If a person aspires to achieve only competent results, then only average and adequate performance should be expected.

Skill

The next phase in the ESPM is the skill level. This is the step that separates the average from the best. A "skill" is the capacity or ability to do something well. Skills are usually acquired or learned, as opposed to abilities, which are often innate or inherited. Advanced skills are usually acquired as a result of experience and/or training and education. Within the skill component, there are different levels of skills, from low to high. One can have minimal skills (above competence) or be highly skilled. Furthermore, if someone wanted to perform as a scientist, physicist, engineer, or another complex role, it would be more advantageous to have a higher aptitude in terms of IQ for complex algorithms and qualitative reasoning. Of course, people can still be scientists or in another mentally challenging field without having a high aptitude or high IQ. However, the pathway to success is much easier with a higher aptitude. One example of how skill impacts success is in the legal field. Although a paralegal is highly knowledgeable in this field compared to a layperson, compared to colleagues like attorneys and judges, the paralegal would be considered at the lower skilled end of the spectrum.

Another example regarding skill would be in the world of golf. I consider myself to be a skilled golfer; however, my playing partners would argue that assertion. Anyway, I've had golf training and coaching, I've had plenty of experience (as I've played on many courses around the world throughout my life), and I generally shoot around a +20 handicap. I know some of you golfers would say that's pretty close to just being competent and not skilled. However, I've played with people who are barely competent at hitting the golf ball but consistently have high scores. The highly skilled golfer would usually be your average pro golfer who can shoot close to par or better most of the time. In contrast to this, I would be considered a lower skilled golfer, and the hacker would be considered barely competent. If you are just learning golf, you need not have the golfing skills in order to participate; however, you will most likely not play particularly well until your skill level increases.

Going back to the typist example as it relates to skill, a competent professional typist is one who can type around 50 WPM. In contrast, skilled professional typists can type from 60 to 120 WPM based on their additional experience and training.

Talent

The final component in the ESPM is talent, or gift. "Talent" is endowment: one is endowed with talent or talents, such as a "gifted" writer who has natural abilities or qualities. This is a person who possesses an unusual, innate ability in some field or activity. Having talent means that for a given activity, job, sport, or professional field, you were born with something special that gives you a slight advantage over the majority of people.

Have you ever noticed how some people seem to be naturally better in certain areas than other people? There are some activities where having a God-given talent can be a huge advantage for the person seeking to perform optimally in that particular activity. Some people were born with a natural ability to sing, whereas others were not. In track, no matter how long and hard I train for the rest of my life, I will not be able to beat Usain Bolt in the one-hundred-meter dash because he is just naturally faster than I am—and apparently everyone else. Some people are gifted public speakers, musicians, computer programmers, artists, mathematicians, scientists, and organizers.

However, having talent doesn't necessarily guarantee you will optimally perform, as you might not utilize that talent to the fullest and will, therefore, miss the opportunity. You may have the talent but not the skill to take advantage of it. Likewise, if you don't have talent, this doesn't mean you can't optimally perform because your high skills along with the other pillar attributes can propel you to perform your best. The most potent performance concoction is to be highly skilled and have natural talent, as that combination is a winning formula if executed properly.

Not everyone is a gifted singer or a skilled public speaker. Therefore, to understand how your God-given talent can be used to optimize your performance, you need to recognize and identify whether or not you have it in the first place. Sometimes we discover our God-given talents through trial and error, and many times we never find it. If you fail in one area, keep searching until you find something you can master.

If you do have the God-given talent in this activity, then use it to your advantage by heavily focusing on the other pillars such as Preparation and Practice. If you don't have it, you'll need to focus on pillars that will help improve your skill level, such as Knowledge (Pillar Three), Practice (Pillar Four), and Communication (Pillar Five). This will give you an amazing ability to overcome any shortcoming.

As far as talent goes, for example, I sing in a men's choir at my church—a wonderful men's choir, I might add. We are separated into different singing sections based on the pitch, tone and the range of our voices. In our choir, we have four sections: first tenors, second tenors, baritones, and basses. When a prospective choir member wants to join the choir, the prospect's voice pitch and tone are thoroughly evaluated to determine the appropriate singing section. For instance, I am a baritone, as that is my God-given voice. There is no sense for me to try to sing tenor or bass, because my voice is not "wired" that way. What comes out of my voice, the sound that I make, is what makes me be me. That is the God-given talent of my voice, that is the profile of my voice, and without surgery or something as drastic as that, I will always have a baritone voice.

What I do with that talent is up to me. Knowing this about my voice, my goal should not be to try to be a great soprano or tenor singer but to become a great baritone singer. Can I use this baritone voice to become a soloist? Can I do all the necessary training to become an optimum-performing baritone singer? This would depend on where I want to go as a choir member. However, the essence of my voice is baritone.

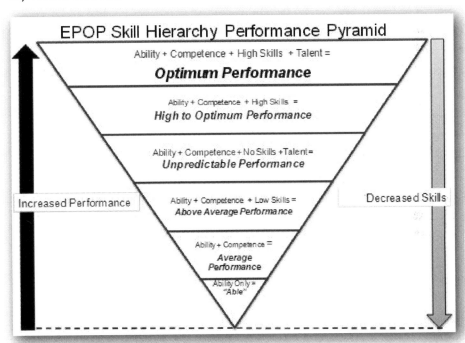

Copyright © 2015 Ainiare Enterprises

Final Thoughts

To get the most out of this Skill Pillar, first find out what your skill level is, and identify any talents you may possess. If you find gaps in ability, competence, or skill, then put together a plan to increase those areas, and fill the gaps. If you discover that you have a unique talent in that area, find out the best way to exploit, utilize, and take advantage of that talent because that will give you an advantage. If you don't have a unique talent, don't be discouraged. Just work hard to increase your skills, and, ultimately, that will lead you to optimally perform.

The optimum performers are the ones who play with the hands that God dealt them, and then build the skills up to optimum levels. From a skill perspective, the key to becoming an optimum performer is to honestly assess your talent in the activity, and then fill in the deficiencies by increasing your skills. The most effective ways to increase your skill set is to learn about new techniques and methods. In short, you need to gain more knowledge that will help you perform more effectively. The next pillar will help bridge the knowledge gap.

CHAPTER 7

He Who Has Knowledge Wins!

Pillar Three: Knowledge

After thoroughly assessing your skill level and determining those areas that need improvement, your next step is to become more knowledgeable about the chosen activity. A major factor in improving and enhancing activity performance is to learn proper techniques and fundamentals. This pillar focuses on improving your knowledge of the targeted subject to help you boost your overall performance.

The famous phrase "knowledge is power" implies that with knowledge or education, training, instruction, coaching, and tutoring, one's potential or abilities in life increase. This is true from an EPOP™ perspective as well. Knowledge is the expertise and skills acquired by a person through experience, education, and/or training. However, knowledge is of no value unless you put it into practice.

I love the game of golf. It is far and away the biggest hobby I have, and it is the activity I'm most passionate about. I've been playing for several years, but when I started playing, I had to learn the hard way that it's more effective to get knowledge, information, and training about something before jumping in headfirst.

In my early golf days, the first thing I did was take some old used clubs to the driving range. At the time, most people believed that golf was difficult to learn and play, as it takes a great deal of preparation, skill, patience, practice, and "thick skin." However, I figured I was different because I was athletic, educated, mentally sound, and smart. What could be so difficult?

During my first venture at the driving range, without receiving any tips or assistance from anyone, I got a bucket of balls and went to work. First, I made sure my new golf outfit was in place. I had a blue Callaway (whatever that was) golf cap with matching pants and a light blue Nike golf shirt. Of course, I had on my $150 pair of golf shoes and $40 golf gloves as well. So I looked like a golfer, I smelled like a golfer, and I had my golf talk and lingo down. Nothing could stop me. What had taken me so long to master this game?

Once I was confident that my golf look and persona was intact, I thought this would be a good time to actually start hitting some balls. So I put the little white ball on this funny-looking rubber thing called a tee. And this rubber tee was sticking up through this fake grass mat. Then I just swung away. After my first swing, I looked up to see where the ball had landed. I thought that I must have hit the ball a long, long way because I couldn't see the ball in the air. So I decided to get another ball and hit it again, but this time I made sure I saw how far it went, which would give me some good bragging stories at the office. To my surprise and embarrassment, the ball was still on the tee staring back up to me, as if to say, "Well, hit me if you can." It hadn't been touched!

What! You gotta be kiddin', I thought and looked around to see if anyone was watching. Thankfully, no one else saw the drastic whiff. I took another hack at the ball, this time with more concentration and focus but less confidence. Swing and a miss; and again, swing and a miss. I couldn't believe that I couldn't hit this still ball sitting on this tee. Finally, in my frustration, I moved the club about six inches from the ball, and then I barely hit it, and the ball went twenty feet sideways.

That was the moment of truth. It was a clear indication that I needed help in the worst way. I finally came to the realization that I was not going to walk on the golf course and play like Tiger Woods in the next couple of days. At the range that day, it was so difficult that I could have been at there for years and still would have been struggling because I didn't know "what" to do and "how" to do it. I could have had all the desire, passion, and focus in the world, but that would not have helped me hit that ball. I could have practiced for the next ten hours, but I would have been wasting time and money (six dollars a bucket) because I would have been practicing bad techniques and methods—because what I was doing was *wrong*. I didn't have what I needed most: knowledge.

I didn't know where to stand. I didn't know how to hold the club. I didn't know which club to use for which situation. And I had no clue how to swing the club properly, as I was swinging at the golf ball as if it were a baseball. I needed to find out more about this game from people who have played it for years and who are good at it.

After my epiphany, I decided to get some of that knowledge. First, I talked to my uncle, who owned and operated a golf shop, and he gave me some initial tips. Then I signed up for beginner's golf lessons at the local golf course. As I got more into the game, I watched it more on TV than I ever did before to help me understand and appreciate it better. In addition, I began reading and subscribing to golf magazines, reading books, watching videos, and searching for information and tips on the "information superhighway" (aka the web, although that's what it was called in the early days).

As my knowledge of the game increased, so did my desire and passion. In turn, my willingness to practice and focus more on golf increased, my overall excitement for the game exploded, and soon after, my execution and results followed with better scores. As my knowledge increased, so did the other pillars. To this day, I'm still in love with and respectful of the game of golf. This love all started by me getting the knowledge I needed to get out of my own way, and then the rest was history.

Getting the Knowledge You Need

In the subject area where you've chosen to optimize performance, it is imperative that you gain as much knowledge from all available sources so that you can ensure you get the most out of the subject. There are a range of methods for getting knowledge, and you need to determine which ones works best for you.

The different sources from which you will be able to attain knowledge will be dependent on your subject or chosen activity, as well as your access to, and the availability of, the resources you need. For some subjects, you may need more knowledge than what you currently possess, but in other cases, you may be starting from "ground zero" in a complex area, so getting all the knowledge you need may take some time.

The diagram below shows some knowledge options available.

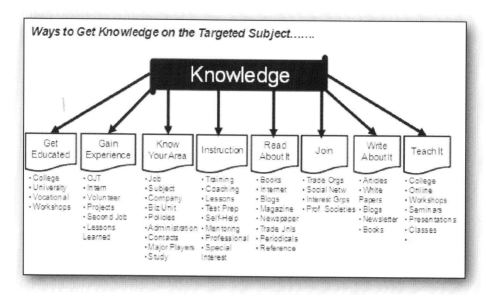

Ways to Get Knowledge on the Targeted Subject.......

Knowledge

Get Educated	Gain Experience	Know Your Area	Instruction	Read About It	Join	Write About It	Teach It
• College	• OJT	• Job	• Training	• Books	• Trade Orgs	• Articles	• College
• University	• Intern	• Subject	• Coaching	• Internet	• Social Netw	• Write	• Online
• Vocational	• Volunteer	• Company	• Lessons	• Blogs	• Interest Grps	Papers	• Workshops
• Workshops	• Projects	• Biz Unit	• Test Prep	• Magazine	• Prof. Societies	• Blogs	• Seminars
	• Second Job	• Policies	• Self-Help	• Newspaper		• Newsletter	• Presentations
	• Lessons Learned	• Administration	• Mentoring	• Trade Jrnls		• Books	• Classes
		• Contacts	• Professional	• Periodicals			
		• Major Players	• Special Interest	• Reference			
		• Study					

Copyright © 2015 Ainiare Enterprises

Get Educated

The most proven method of increasing knowledge to improve overall perfor-mance is through education. Aside from gaining knowledge and improving per-formance, getting educated has numerous other benefits. According to a 2007 study called "Education Pays" by Sandy Baum and Jennifer Ma, the benefits of higher education for individuals and for society as a whole are both monetary and nonmonetary (Baum and Ma 2007). Higher levels of education lead to both higher levels of earnings individually and higher tax revenues for federal, state, and local governments. The study also claims that the typical bachelor's degree recipient can expect to earn about 61 percent more over a forty-year working life than the typical high-school graduate earns over the same period. In addition, unemploy-ment rates are much lower for college graduates than for high-school graduates. Also, higher family-income levels, higher parent-education levels, and higher test scores are all associated with higher degree-completion rates for students enrolled in four-year colleges and universities.

In the mid-1990s, I had a golf-catalog business that sold golf-training aids. As a passionate but somewhat average golfer, I knew the golf side of the business very well. Where I was really challenged was on the business side of things. My challenges were specifically in the business areas of marketing, operations, finance, administration, overall strategy, and business planning. My experience helped me to quickly realize that if I was to really try to grow a business and be successful, then I should seek some more education in the area. I decided to go to school to get my MBA.

However, before I really learned my lesson, I thought I'd take another shot at running a business without any real knowledge. Since I had a master's degree in software engineering and plenty of industry software development and programming experience, I started a software development company. At the time, I thought I had all the elements needed to run the company. I knew the technology, and I had vast technical experience and training. However, as much as I knew about the technical side, it was the exact opposite on the business side. I failed to realize the importance of such things as how to bill and invoice customers, how to make sure the phones were answered when I was not in the office, and how to factor in taxes, depreciation, overhead, and expenses. In short, I needed to know how business worked.

That is when I decided to go get my MBA so I could gain more of understanding and structured knowledge about the business area. College is a great way to attain education, whether you go for a two-year AA degree, four-year Bachelor of Science or arts degree, or graduate degree.

Besides the degree, college allows you to show to the world and to yourself that you can complete something. It teaches you how to finish. It also makes you well rounded, and not only in the subject matter that you are looking for. For instance, for a business degree, you also need to take English, writing, and math. All those components help make you a better overall individual while building your particular area of expertise.

Formal education also helps you improve your social and group skills. In college, you need to work with all different types of people, different races, and different types of teachers. Sometimes you have to do projects within small or large groups, and you quickly learn about the different dynamics of working with people. You will find out the circumstances in which you are naturally a leader, and those in which you are comfortable just being a team member. You will also, in all likelihood, have an experience where members of the group do not do a lot of work at all, and you have to figure out how to make that work.

An education helps you improve your overall communication abilities including written, oral, and presentation skills. You normally have to do a lot of report and essay writing, as well as put together presentations and speak in front of the class. You will also improve time-management skills, as you will have to meet deadlines and milestones, and there are consequences when you do not meet those. This forces you to put a plan together, work toward that plan, meet that plan, and make those things happen.

Higher Education

Within the EPOP™ approach, getting educated means that after high school, you participate in and finish some type of formal higher-education program. Higher education is about taking your education to the optimum level. The goal of the higher education program you choose is to provide you with the tools, knowledge, and core competencies you need to get where you want to be. These higher-education programs may consist of at least one of the following education pathways:

- vocational schools
- community college
- university
- institute of technology
- specialized schools
- academies (i.e., military)

There are several pathways to getting the education that will lead to different types of diplomas, depending on the degree of education. Getting a formal education can take anywhere from six months to ten years.

When you finish vocational school, you do not get a degree. Instead, you get a certificate, which is necessary to practice some careers. For instance, a vocational school can train you in certain medical or dental careers, such as a lab technician. You will get a certificate, but you will also need to pass an exam to get licensed.

The targeted degree at community colleges is an associate of arts degree (called an AA). An AA is designed to be completed within two years; however, most participants take longer. A bachelor of arts (BA) or bachelor of science (BS) degree can be achieved by completing a four-year college or university.

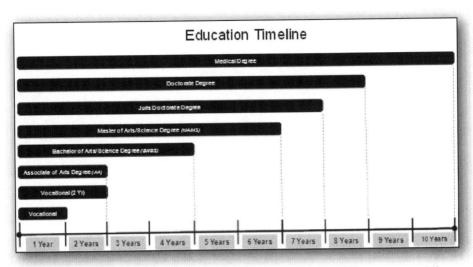

Vocational Schools

In addition to colleges and city colleges, vocational schools are viable education alternatives. Vocational schools teach you hands-on career skills, from driving a giant diesel truck to the specific skills you need to become a welder, cosmetologist, electronic technician, or chef.

A vocational school is different from a four-year college. It is basically an abbreviated way to get a degree. Where formal university may take four to five years to complete, a vocational completion will take six months to two years to get a certificate. The curriculum mainly focuses on specific skills for specific jobs, such as for the following:

- auto and boat mechanic
- blacksmithing
- bridal consultant
- carpentry
- electricians
- floral design
- home inspection
- hotel and restaurant management
- locksmithing
- medical billing

- medical insurance
- medical-office assistant
- medical transcription
- motorcycle-repair technician
- plumbing
- retail
- technology
- veterinary assistant
- welding

These schools are sometimes the best way for adults to reenter the job market and are also a great way for high-school graduates who want to take accelerated routes to specific careers, rather than going to more general universities. Vocational school graduates can be prepared to take high-paying, skilled jobs immediately upon graduation.

Colleges

In the United States, the word "college" and "university" are loosely interchangeable, although in many other countries, college may refer to a secondary or high school. For this discussion, "college" will be used to mean any postsecondary, undergraduate education.

Colleges vary in terms of size, degree, and length of stay. Two-year colleges (although, most never finish in two years) are also known as junior or community colleges. These colleges are usually used to get an associate's degree (AA), which can be transferred to a university (or four-year college) or to get a certificate of some kind (similar to vocational schools).

Generally, community colleges typically offer six facets of education:

1. Transfer Education: the traditional two-year student who will then transfer to a four-year institution to pursue a BS/BA degree
2. Career Education: the traditional two-year student who will graduate with an AA degree and directly enter the workforce
3. Developmental Education: remedial education for high-school graduates who are not academically ready to enroll in college-level courses
4. Continuing Education: noncredit courses offered to the community for personal development and interest

5. Industry Training: contracted training and education wherein a local company pays the college to provide specific training or courses for their employees
6. E-Learning: distance learning online using one's computer and proctored exams

Universities

Similar to colleges, universities are postsecondary institutions of higher education that primarily grant four-year and graduate degrees. A university provides both undergraduate and postgraduate education.

Regarding EPOP™, knowledge will be enhanced via the university route, as gaining a degree can significantly increase and improve career advancement opportunities. Also, if you want to change careers, there are a wider variety of career options to choose from. In addition, with a degree or additional or advanced degrees, you are most likely to progress much faster up the career ladder.

In addition to knowledge, you will develop core competencies at the university. Universities can teach you how to research, collect, dissect, analyze, filter, interpret, and report information.

Gain Experience

On-the-Job Training

Another important way to gain knowledge is through experience. Sometimes it is better to go through something once to learn about it. You can often read something in a book, but you still don't thoroughly understand how it works until you actually try it or experience it. It's important to "go through the motions" to get a feeling of how something works. Once you get the experience, you have a better perspective on how to improve your performance in that area.

In fact, it is sometimes better to fail at something so you have a better appreciation of what you should *not* do next time, rather than getting everything right all the time. Many famous entrepreneurs have failed several times in business ventures before hitting it big, as they continued to learn how to get things accomplished by going through the experience several times.

Have you noticed that star collegiate athletes normally have challenges during the first couple of years as professionals? It's often difficult to adjust to the professional level due to their lack of experience. However, once they continue to get the experience and enhance their learning, they become more effective professionals.

Interning

As mentioned in the beginning of the book, we no longer live in a flat, less competitive world, and the job market is much more challenging these days. It is no longer good enough to simply be better than your local college mates. An effective way to get the upper hand on your competitors is to intern.

Graduating students with internships on their résumés, compensated or not, are more likely to get full-time jobs upon graduation. The reason is that the interns now have track records, and most hiring managers like to reduce their risks.

Volunteering

Volunteering is another valuable way to get work experience in many different industries. This type of experience enables you to learn, pick up, and enhance new skills by trying different and unique jobs. When you volunteer, the community wins, and you benefit from your experiences. Through your experience, you might find something you'd enjoy doing permanently or discover what you don't want to pursue. In addition, volunteering can help you meet people who may be in positions to assist you when you are looking for a paid position.

Taking on Projects

A surefire way to gain knowledge and experience, especially at corporate-level companies, is to take on extra projects or tasks. In this current work environment, people are being laid off by the thousands. If you can do something to stand out in a positive way, your chances of staying with the company should increase. If it happens to be a project that is worthwhile to the company, then you might be able to stay on to manage or work on the project.

In addition to saving yourself from layoffs, creating or taking on projects can help you learn and pick up valuable experience that you can use for your current job and a future job, if necessary. Taking on projects can also help to build up skill sets and establish relationships.

A Second Job

Another effective way to increase your knowledge is to take a second job in the area you desire. In addition to gaining knowledge, a second job can help you gain additional contacts and build your network while putting extra funds in your pocket. Also, a second job can help you stay active in a target industry by continuously developing your skills.

For people who have challenges finding work—such as recent graduates, people looking to change careers, people looking to enhance their careers, or people jump-starting their current careers—a second job can help them add experience to their résumés. If you are starting a business, and you are not totally comfortable with all the processes and operations involved in making the business work, a second job in the field is a great way to evaluate if that field is the right place for you. With that type of experience at hand, you can gain insight into what makes this business or field unique. Exploring different parts of the business allows you to get a different perspective of the field and helps you understand the process much better.

Know Your Area

To gain more knowledge that will help you perform better in a certain subject or activity, you simply need to know your area and its basic attributes. Know the area or the activity or the sport you are engaged in.

For instance, if you want to perform better in your job, just knowing the simplest things about that job will be paramount in helping you be more successful. Make a point of gaining knowledge about your company including its history, mission, goals, targets, overall strategy, and financial status. When you know about these particular areas, you are better able to maneuver around your work arena. You also need to know the various business units and departments, different teams and what they are comprised of, and the overall structure of how that all works.

Specifically, you need to know the policies, processes, procedures, and overall culture of that environment. The policies, processes, and procedures are the basic rules you must abide by in your workplace or in your business. Knowing the specific culture is also important. For instance, if the culture is quiet or deals with high-level and affluent people, then you don't want to go out in the hall screaming. Knowing the culture helps you act appropriately.

Another thing to know involves administrative functions, or how things generally work. Most importantly, you need to know how human resources functions in your workplace and what applies to you. For instance, what is the office dress code? Do you come in suits, or do you dress business casual? How do different functions work, such as accounts payable, purchasing, facilities management, and payroll? Make it a point to know what type of security there is. All of this will make perform your job better.

You should also know the contacts, those people who will help you get where you want to go, get the answers you need, and get the results that you are trying to achieve. You also need to know the major players in this. Who can really get things done in your workplace? Who are the gatekeepers? Who are the vice presidents, the presidents, and the people who are the big decision makers in the business? Who are the deal makers, the ones who can get you to the person who can do the deal? Who are the major players who make things happen?

Instruction

Another key way to get knowledge on a particular subject matter or activity is to take special classes. You can take these to improve overall performance as well as focus on things you want to get better at.

One popular area in which to take special classes is standardized test preparation. For instance, if you are a student, and you are taking the SAT exam, a preparation class provides an effective way to acquire valuable information, knowledge, and high performance tips. Attending these preparation classes will usually enhance performance success. Preparation classes also work well for other standardized exams, such as the Graduate Record Examination (GRE), the Graduate management Admissions Test (GMAT), the Law School Admission Test (LSAT), and many more.

Special classes are also useful when taking technical or professional exams such as the Cisco Certified Network Associate (CCNA®), the Project Management Professional (PMP), Information Technology Infrastructure Library (ITIL), and Microsoft and Cisco certification exams. Special classes can help acquire performance enhancing test taking skills and unique tips to help better and improve your performance.

Another instruction area is computer-based training. Here, you can go on the web and learn the subject matter. Instruction, and then some sample tests, scores, and feedback are usually available. DVDs are another learning option. These are usually packed with a whole library of different references, information, and sample tests.

Another good option is to take lessons. This is especially valuable in areas such as sports and music. Find a good teacher who comes highly recommended. The teacher will help you gain knowledge and improve your skills all the way down the line.

You might also improve your knowledge by going into training or getting coached. A good coach will push you and perhaps even develop drills that will allow you to really get how to do the activity in your mind. It is sometimes better to work with a coach, because this is an outside person pushing you to do something rather than you pushing yourself. For instance, you might get tired when you are doing your exercises. You might do fifteen push-ups on your own, but a trainer can push you to twenty-five (where probably thought you couldn't even do twenty). But they are able to get that out of you.

A coach or trainer is also knowledgeable and will know some of the proper exercises that can work for your particular body. For instance, a golf trainer can look at your swing and tell you if it is not correct. You sometimes can't do this by yourself because you can't see it, you do not have the expertise, and thus you cannot critique yourself. It is often better to get a coach or trainer who can push you to go to past the limits that you normally would push for yourself.

Read about It

Of course, since you are reading this book, you are definitely aware that one of the easiest and most prevalent ways to gain knowledge quickly and effectively is by reading. The trick is finding the most impactful and efficient thing to read. The traditional method for gaining knowledge through reading is via books, magazines, trade journals, reference texts, newspapers, and periodicals.

In addition to those traditional methods, valuable knowledge can be gained from reading content on the Internet, specifically digital articles retrieved through the various search engines. In addition, reading blogs on specific topics can also be useful.

Internet Search Engines, Gateway Websites, and Social Networking

The Internet is fabulous, and you can read about practically any subject matter. It is easy to find information on whatever subject you want using any of the major search engines. The Internet is your friend, and you need to embrace it. If you want to compete and get the same type of information as other people, get it quickly,

JEFF FREEMAN MBA, PMP

and get it efficiently, then you need to utilize the Internet. The days of not trusting the Internet are gone, and if you feel that way, then you are going to be left behind.

Another area on the Internet where a wealth of knowledge is shared is through social networking. You can go to Facebook, Twitter, or Instagram to find information about your particular subject and see what other people are talking about.

You can also go to subject-matter websites that are specifically targeted for that particular topic. For instance, if you wanted to know anything about the government and the way it works, there are specific websites where you can find this information.

So the Internet is wonderful and often has all the information you need for any topic. However, you need to be aware that not all websites have credible and accurate information, so choose your online sources carefully. For more suggestions on choosing the correct internet source, please refer to (UW Green Bay, 2014).

Blogs

One other source to look at is blogs, which are a personal kind of Internet journal, and they are taking the Internet to a whole new level. Everyone and anyone have blogs on a plethora of different subjects. Some blogs are more accurate than others, so you need to be careful.

Different bloggers write about different things. Bloggers are sort of like newspaper columnists, but they may not have college degrees or training in the area they are writing about. They just believe they have enough background to communicate their experiences, and you take them for what they're worth.

Books, Magazines, and Journals

Don't forget about the old "tried and true" source of knowledge: books. This approach to learning has been used for thousands of years, long before the computer, Internet, search engines, social networks, and blogs arrived on the scene. Books are obviously the most reliable, tested, and stable method available to provide the knowledge and information you need on a particular topic. You can buy books at a brick-and-mortar store (the actual store that you walk into, similar to a Barnes & Noble or Borders store, or any other bookstore in the mall). You can go to a library and get books as well, of course.

You can also get books online in one of two ways. You can order hard copies at one of the major book websites, like Amazon.com or Barnesandnoble.com, where you can have the book delivered to your home or place of business or wherever you like. Or you can buy the e-book, where you can download the contents of the book so you have an electronic version either on your computer or on an e-reader such as the Kindle from Amazon or the Nook from Barnes & Noble. You can also download the e-book on other devices such as your smartphone, iPad, or tablet.

You can also read about a particular subject matter or activity in magazines and newspaper articles. Some magazines are written specifically for certain activities. For instance, if you are into running, there are particular magazines geared toward that specific topic. You can also read or subscribe to trade journals about the subject matter you are interested in.

So reading is a great place to find information on any type of subject matter, whether it's related to work, business, school, sports, or home.

Join Organizations

Another great way to gain knowledge is to join different organizations that cater to targeted subject matter. You can even join these groups online through social networking sites like Facebook and LinkedIn. These groups host ongoing conversations about the topic and have conferences about it as well. In the technology world, there are all sorts of interest groups that you can join in any particular area to help you learn about the subject matter.

You can also join trade organizations, which is a great way to pick up knowledge. There are also often industry workshops, seminars, and conferences available, where you can attend numerous lectures from some of the leaders in the field. For instance, there are leaders in the corporate world who can direct you on how to handle your corporate setting and management. Leaders in business can tell you how to become a better entrepreneur, how to invest, how to look for angel funding. There are seminars on everything you can think of, and so, this is a great way to learn about different topics and get knowledge on a particular subject.

Write about It

Writing about something is another key way to pick up information and become more knowledgeable on a particular area. You can write white papers, articles, blog posts, and/or you can write a book. When you join one of the above organizations, and you think that you can offer something, you may be asked to write up a particular white paper for your peers. Another great writing option is to start a blog. As you research in preparation to write, you then become more knowledge-able because you are now required to convey accurate information, and you know you have got to get your facts straight.

Teach It

I learned at an early age that another way to pick up knowledge is to teach or tu-tor the topic to others. When I was in college, I tutored calculus and trigonometry. Even though I did pretty well in those classes as a student, I had to be extremely knowledgeable in order to teach the concepts, theories, and practical applications to other college students. The more I tutored, the sharper I became in math, sci-ence, and engineering as a whole.

One of the reasons I became a college professor teaching project management was to learn more about that field. Teaching the subject was the best way for me to understand the concepts in order to explain them to someone else.

Teaching and tutoring forced me to work harder to understand the material, recall it more accurately, and apply the concepts and learning more effectively. In short, if you want to be an optimum performer in something, teach that something to others.

Knowledge Pillar Final Thoughts

In the previous chapter, Skill Pillar, we understood the importance of recognizing, iden-tifying, and assessing our skill level for a particular activity. Through that assessment, we can identify how skilled we are in an activity, and we can also highlight areas that need to be further enriched and improved in order to optimize overall performance.

In this chapter, Knowledge Pillar, we learned how to improve skill gaps through various techniques, training, coaching, and education.

Once we gain the knowledge needed to improve, the next chapter, Practice Pillar, will help us learn how to solidify and engrain these newfound knowledge tech-niques and learning into our skill set, which will further help the road to perfor-mance optimization.

CHAPTER 8

Practice till You Can't Go Any Further; Then Do One More

Pillar Four: Practice

Vince Lombardi said, "Practice does not make perfect. Only perfect practice makes perfect." The importance of practicing, and practicing effectively, is the primary focus of this pillar. Being able to incorporate an effective practice routine into your overall performance strategy will reap positive results toward achieving optimum performance in whatever you are trying to accomplish.

One of the most famous practice quotes comes from classical pianist Arthur Rubinstein. As the story is told, he was approached in the street near Carnegie Hall in New York by a man who asked, "Pardon me, sir, but how do I get to Carnegie Hall?" to which Rubinstein replied, "Practice!"

This very important pillar focuses on the power of practice. Practice and repetition are the keys to ensuring preparation is applied, skills are appropriate utilized, and knowledge gains are not wasted. Practice is the key to achieving optimum results after the first three pillars have been properly explored and utilized. After you've gained the appropriate knowledge via education, training, or any other means described in the knowledge pillar, and you have embedded the proper techniques into your cranium, body, and soul, it's now time for you to practice what you've learned.

Practicing is mandatory if you want to be an optimum performer. You can possess all the skill and talent in the world, you can prepare and plan for years, and you can get world-class, exclusive, one-of-a-kind training and schooling, but if you don't practice what you have gained, then all of that knowledge will go to waste. Every champion or great in any discipline (sports, business, or entertainment) practices long and hard. Usually the amount of practice time people put in is what separates them from the competition.

In an elite setting where the competition is stiff (such as with world-class Olympic athletes, high-achiever groups, and top sales people), the difference between being good versus being great frequently comes down to who studies the hardest, who practices the most, and who puts in the extra work to go beyond the average call of duty. Due to equivalent skill sets, everyone on the top has the same access to education, training, and coaching. Thus, their ultimate success is often determined by how much each practices and applies repetitive techniques.

The successful optimum performers are the ones who take the time to practice their craft more than the other competitors. These are the ones who frequently come to practice early and stay late afterward. They are "those" employees who go home or to the library after work to study and practice presentations or sales pitches when other office mates are at the bar or watching TV at home. Olympic athletes are known to practice several hours a day for the majority of the year for several years.

Champions such as pro golfers Phil Mickelson and Tiger Woods, basketball Hall-of-Famer Magic Johnson, sales icon and motivational speaker Zig Ziglar, music legend Michael Jackson, film director James Cameron, and even reality-contest winners on *Dancing with the Stars* and *American Idol* practice, practice, practice until they are sick and tired of practicing. Then they practice some more. Optimum performers, great performers, and winning performers practice until it hurts, and then they go to sleep, wake up, and start practicing again and again until the knowledge is ingrained and embedded into their fibers, their cores, and their minds. That's what winners, champions, and optimum performers do.

In short, you will increase your chances of attaining optimum performance through diligent hard work and repetitive practice over time. As explained in the Skills Pillar, skills and talent will only get you so far.

Perhaps the best NBA basketball player ever, Michael Jordan has also been called the best and most intense *practice* player ever as well. According to many published reports, he was always the first one on the practice floor and the last one to leave. He was known to practice all day and into the night. Although he was a superstar, rich, and famous, he also had the skill, talent, desire, experience, and knowledge of the game. He still practiced harder, longer, and more competitively during practice than almost anyone else.

He performed each practice drill as if he was in a game. By practicing this way, he prepared himself to always respond at game-level speed and in game situations. That way, when he encountered that sane situation in a game, he had conditioned himself to react appropriately. By practicing hard at game speed all the time, he prepared himself to execute during the game at a higher level and intensity than most other players.

You can use this philosophy in your daily life, such as when studying for an exam, doing a presentation or sales pitch, practicing an instrument, or just preparing to run a 5K. Try to take it up a notch and practice and train like it is the actual event, and you will get better results when the event *does* happen.

According to the article "Secrets of Greatness" by Geoffrey Colvin, hard work, practice, and dedication are also critical to success many fields. In a study of twenty-year-old violinists by Ericsson and colleagues, the best group (judged by conservatory teachers) averaged ten thousand hours of deliberate practice over their lives; the next best averaged seventy-five hundred hours; and the next, five thousand. It's the same story in surgery, insurance sales, and virtually every sport. More deliberate practice equals better performance. Tons of it equals great performance (Colvin 2006).

There is no substitute for hard work; nobody is great without it. There is no shortcut around it. It simply takes hard work to be an optimum performer or any type of positive performer, for that matter. There is no replacement for it. It is simply about getting down and putting forth an effort to get the job done. There's no evidence of high-level performance without experience or practice. Rather, there is a notion that even top-performing people need around ten years of hard work before becoming world class; this is commonly called the "ten-year rule."

It would be nice to believe that there is a field, industry, or discipline where you may be naturally gifted and that those gifts alone will propel you to greatness and optimum success. However, in the majority of cases, it just doesn't happen that way. In order to be great, you have to practice, and you have to put in the hard work.

Many athletes are legendary for their brutal, rigorous practice routines or their practice discipline. As mentioned earlier, in the case of Michael Jordan, he practiced intensely. In fact, since Michael Jordan was so great in basketball, it's hard to fathom that basketball did not come as a natural, great gift for him. But he was actually cut from his high-school basketball team. Yet through his hard work, effort, diligence, and a very large chip on his shoulder, he got through and became the legend he is today.

Jerry Rice, who is arguably the greatest receiver in NFL history and could possibly be the greatest player period, was passed up by several teams during the NFL draft. Although he had a fantastic senior season at Mississippi Valley State College, many teams weren't sold on him, as many considered him too slow or felt that he did not have the right hands to be a quality professional receiver. Only two teams were seriously interested in drafting him: Dallas and San Francisco. San Francisco ended up taking him as the sixteenth pick in the first round. However, the lack of serious interest gave Jerry Rice the determination to show the other teams what they had missed.

To erase any doubt about his readiness and ability to compete week in and week out, Jerry Rice was dedicated to preparation and practice. In fact, his training routines were the stuff of legend, where he would do hill sprints for two and a half miles up while racing against the clock. He invited other players to practice with him, so a lot of guys joined him in his hill-and-mountain training. But they could not keep up because he had a rigorous practice routine, and, after a few sessions with him, they never came back.

Actual team training camp did not match up to Jerry Rice's routine, as he had already prepared himself optimally. So when it came time to actually execute and play games, he was several steps ahead of the competition in every game due to his rigorous practice and preparation routine. This led him to be a consistent optimum performer every year while building a Hall-of-Fame career.

My favorite athlete is Tiger Woods. Despite his personal challenges several years ago, Tiger is an optimum performer in all the pillars, including this Practice Pillar. Tiger is a prime example of someone who was very talented but got to greatness because of his hard work and practice regimen.

Tiger's father introduced him to golf at an extremely early age: eighteen months. And when Tiger was old enough, he was encouraged to practice intensely. As a youth, he had already racked up at least fifteen years of practice, and at that time, he became the youngest-ever winner of the US Amateur Championship at the age of eighteen. Of course, there were other kids there who had great talent and the best coaches money could buy, but sometimes what separates people is the hard work that is put in, and Tiger has always been dedicated to practice.

You also have to be committed to the time you spend practicing whatever activity you choose. Ed Macauley, a legendary NBA and ABA basketball player, once said, "When you are not practicing, remember someone, somewhere is practicing, and when you meet him, he will win."

Integrating a Sound Practice Regimen

Practicing and studying hard will sometimes cause you to push beyond your normal limits in order to achieve optimum success. However, you have to do whatever it takes to get the job done. Many times, you have to wake up early and stay up late. You have to push aside the urge to sleep when you have deadlines. Sometimes you have to say no to parties. These are just some of the areas in the Practice Pillar that you must commit to in order to become an optimum performer.

Within this pillar, we will explore how to integrate a sound practice regimen and routine into your daily life, just like Michael Jordan, Jerry Rice, and Tiger Woods. You can start by using the following practice steps:

1. Identify and utilize practice schemes.
2. Incorporate practice habits.
3. Develop studying techniques.
4. Take breaks the proper way.

Practice Schemes

Practicing will be more successful when you understand the practice environments that enable you to be more effective. When practicing, one of the key things to focus on is identifying, selecting, and utilizing a practice scheme that works for *you.*

There are several practice schemes that help enrich your practice routines:

1. practice to improve
2. repetition
3. muscle-memory building
4. sectional repetition
5. deliberate practice
6. flash cards
7. target notes
8. rehearsal

9. outside the box
10. Take practice tests - continuously push yourself through practice tests
11. self-assessment
12. metrics and feedback

Practice to Improve
NHL hockey player great Eric Lindros once said, "It's not necessarily the amount of time you spend at practice that counts; it's what you put into practice." Don't practice just for the sake of practicing. Practice with the goal of trying to improve overall performance. The goal of "practice to improve" is to consistently, methodically, and gradually strengthen performance beyond current levels. Understand that you cannot just put in time and expect to significantly get better. You have to consistently stretch and push yourself during practice sessions. Once you stretch yourself as far as you can go, push even further and harder.

You need to go hard when you practice, not just go through the motions to get the practice session over with. You need to max out and put your effort into it. This way, when it's time to execute, you have already put in your best effort, and execution hopefully becomes easier.

Gauge the practice effectiveness and performance improvement by setting up informal and formal milestones. These milestones should be represented by three levels:

1. threshold
2. target
3. stretch

The *threshold* is the minimal goal you are trying to reach. It is the mark that you want to ensure you do not go below, as if this happens you will not be able to reach your ultimate overall objective. The *target* is the mark above the threshold and is considered the improvement milestone. Once achieved, it is a practice indicator that shows progress and performance improvement above the threshold, and is usually moved higher until a level of performance is reached. The *stretch* is the mark that at first appears unattainable; however, if it's reached, you have greatly exceeded your overall goals.

For instance, imagine you are currently practicing to eventually run the 5K (assume it is exactly three miles) and have already managed to complete the distance in thirty-six minutes (twelve minutes per mile). Say you wanted to improve that time to thirty minutes. Then the new threshold you would need to reach for each mile is ten minutes per mile. However, if you wanted to push yourself a little more to ensure you achieve the goal consistently and reliably, you might set a target of perhaps nine minutes per mile. If you are able to consistently achieve that target during practice, then you would be more confident during the actual run.

If you are consistently hitting the target in practice, you may want to see how much you can really stretch yourself, and you may set a stretch target of seven minutes per mile. With this stretch target, you constantly strive to improve your performance even though you may not be able to hit it. But you never know unless you try. Constantly try to push yourself while you're practicing. Find out where your threshold is. Find out of how far you can push to get your target. Try to find your personal breaking point, your stretch.

Here's another example. When doing homework for school, try to answer the challenging problems in the textbook at the end of the chapter rather than skipping over them. When you continue to stretch yourself in that manner, you will better prepare yourself for the actual exam. This is improving as you practice.

Mahatma Gandhi once said, "Practice as if you are the worst; perform as if you are the best." When you put yourself in the mind-set that you are the worst in the field or have the lowest test scores or are the worst shooter or golfer, the goal for you would be to vigorously practice to improve identified deficiencies and gaps that are obstacles to optimum performance. However, when you actually perform, approach the activity like you are the best.

If you are on a team (any type of team), imagine that you are the worst-performing teammate (even if you are actually the best, like Michael Jordan). Then you will work extra hard during practice, put in more effort, and focus on becoming the top-performing team member. When it is time to perform, execute with that same intensity and effort, and you will usually outperform most competitors who did not work as hard in practice.

Repetition

Another valuable practice scheme is repetition. Through repetition, the goal is to build muscle memory and memorization skills. Martha Graham, who was a famous dance choreographer back in the early twentieth century, said, "Practice means to perform over and over again in the face of all obstacles, some act of vision, of faith, of desire. Practice is a means of inviting the perfection desired." She went on to say, "I am a dancer. I believe we learn by practice. Whether it means to learn to dance by practicing dancing or to learn to live by practicing living, the principles are the same." This great statement basically shows that repetition, or practicing over and over again until you get it right, is a key ingredient to success. Even if you think you know the activity, you owe it to yourself to practice it more than once, as your chance for success increases each time you go through the activity. Even though you may have nailed it that first time, go back, and try to nail it again. If you can do that, repeat your best practice performance at least ten more times. Repetition is all about doing something over and over until you get it right, and then doing it again.

Build Muscle Memory

Muscle memory, also known as motor learning, is another way to utilize the power of repetition. It's a form of procedural memory that involves consolidating a specific motor task into your memory through repetition. Huh? Well, basically muscle memory is developed by going over something repetitively until it becomes routine for that particular muscle. When a movement is repeated over time, the long-term muscle memory is created for that particular task. Eventually, this will allow a person to perform without a conscious effort. This process decreases the need for attention and creates maximum efficiency within the motor and memory systems. Bike riding, typing, playing video games, and playing an instrument are all examples of muscle-memory activities.

Memorization is the key to building that muscle memory. You need to memorize things over and over again to get them ingrained at that level.

Sectional Repetition

Sectional repetition allows you to split the entire work of the activity into mini practice or study sections rather than studying or practicing the entire activity at one time. For example, when my son was in elementary school, he was required to take a states test. He needed to learn all fifty states and identify each one on the larger map of the United States. When my son started studying, he tried to learn all fifty states at one time. However, when he got to the thirtieth state or so, he would forget the next states because it was too much to learn at one time. So we broke the states into sections of ten for him, and he learned and memorized each section until he mastered it. Once he mastered all the sections, he would go over the activity as a whole. Using this method, he studied and memorized the states efficiently and effectively without frustration. He got 100 percent on the test each year.

Sectional repetition can also be applied when studying multichapter exams when you are in school. If a final exam is on four chapters, don't try to read through all four at once. Using sectional repetition, study each chapter separately and repetitively until you master its contents. After mastering the chapter, go to the next.

Likewise, when practicing golf on the driving range, don't practice hitting the golf balls by taking out each club and hitting the ball with each club. The most effective way to go to the driving range is to use sectional repetition by taking out one club at a time and practicing with that club until you are satisfied with your progress. Then you put that club back in the bag, pull out another, and repeat the cycle. Similarly, if you are doing a speech at work, break the speech down into sections to get that speech going, and then practice the entire speech.

Deliberate Practice

Deliberate practice is a practice scheme where the "practice makes perfect" saying comes into play. More deliberate practice equals better performance. Tons of it equals great performance (Colvin 2006). With deliberate practice, it is not enough to just practice; you have to practice the proper techniques. And you need to practice in a manner that will help you improve. With deliberate practice, you get instant and continuous feedback on your practice or study session and provide feedback as well. As you continue practicing in a deliberate fashion, you can use that feedback to continue to get better. In addition, through this type of practice, you set goals, objectives, and targets that will enable you to more accurately monitor your practice or study session. Once you get feedback on the practice results, make adjustments, if necessary. Then keep practicing deliberately until you achieve your goals or targets.

Deliberate practice is an activity explicitly intended to help you improve your performance; it enables you to reach for objectives that are beyond what you are normally capable of doing. The goal of deliberate practice is to make your practice time more efficient and effective. When you start deliberate practicing, you need to be fully absorbed in and focused on practicing so that you can be truly effective. The optimum performers in any field are those who subconsciously or consciously deliberate practice.

Again using golf as an example, to practicing golf most people go to the driving range. However, many golfers do not have a practice plan. They basically get a bucket of balls, go to their golf mat, and just hit the balls randomly until there are none left in the bucket. Practicing that way does not provide the best method to determine if you are improving.

In contrast, when you deliberate practice at the golf range, you practice with goals or targets in mind. For example, you can target practice with the flags using the correct club that would normally be used to reach that flag. You can aim for the flag and determine your accuracy. As you hit the golf balls for the flag, you can see where the ball is landing. Is the ball left or right, short or long? With that information and feedback, you can adjust your club or swing to zero in on the target. Once you have consistently hit the target, you can set goals to hit it ten times, five straight times, or something similar. Try hitting the flagstick, or try to leave the ball five to six feet in putting range. Continue to practice hitting until the correct precision is achieved.

Of course, when I practice golfing, I don't do all that, but pro golfers use deliberate practicing all the time. So by continuously observing, having goals, making the proper adjustments, and doing it repetitiously and repeatedly every day, you are deliberate practicing.

Flash Cards

Flash cards are a powerful study tool that can be used for homework, tests, and, presentations (they are not particularly useful for sports). To use flash cards, write the answer on one side and the question on the other, and then test yourself. Practice the flash cards continuously until you get all of them right.

If you do not get the answer, put that flash card to the left, and if you get the answer right put it to the right, and keep going. At the end, go back, and study the ones you got wrong intensively. Once you think you know everything, put all the cards back into one stack, and then do it again. Once you get the entire stack right, and then study them ten more times.

Study Target Notes

In the early part of my college years, I was so excited about being in college and learning about all this new stuff like philosophy, psychology, and art that I wanted to read each textbook cover to cover. When I studied for tests, I read the entire chapter, as I thought I needed to know everything about the subject. However, I usually ran out of time and couldn't thoroughly grasp the subject matter for a test because I had only read it once. As you might imagine, my test scores weren't very good during that period.

As time went on, and I saw other people getting higher scores, I asked them how they did it. I said, "How did you read the book that fast?" They said, "Book? Is there a book for this class?" Then they explained that all they studied were the specific notes for the class that the instructor provided.

It is an unspoken rule that if an instructor spends valuable time on specific topics, you should be keenly aware that those topics will likely be on the exam. The notes provided by the instructor, trainer, or mentor are the "target" notes that you should study and really know if you wanted to get the highest possible scores. Of course, back in college I still read the book, but I just read whatever complemented the notes and lecture provided by the instructor. Do not just study anything that is out there. Study particular target notes, and this will help you focus on what you are trying to achieve.

Rehearse

Rehearse whatever you are doing. If it is a speech, rehearse, rehearse, and rehearse. If it is in music, then rehearse how you will play that particular piece for the recital. If you need to do a presentation, rehearse it over and over.

Try acting it out in the mirror. Look at yourself, see how you look, see your face, hear your voice, and hear your inflections. Or practice with a partner. Act it out with a friendly audience using people who will pay attention and do their best to help you.

Think Outside the Box

Sometimes in order to get the most out of a practice session, you must try a different or unique approach, as traditional practice methods may not be effective for the current situation. In those cases, it might be appropriate and more effective to think outside the box. Try different things, and you might come up with a new way of approaching something.

In the movie called *Drumline*, starring Nick Cannon, a young man tries to fit into a band at school. This character is sort of a prima donna and thinks he knows everything about playing the drums. He thinks he doesn't need to practice basic techniques, and he is at odds with the music's traditional style and the overall direction of the band and its leaders. He refuses to be a team player. One thing leads to another, and he eventually gets kicked out of the band.

While out of the band, the main character reflects on how he misses the band camaraderie and companionship. However, he still feels the band's music and style needs a facelift. So he comes up with an out-of-the-box idea to spice up the band to make it more contemporary while keeping the traditional feel the director desires. To convince the band leaders of his idea, he gets together with some other team members and puts together a composed out-of-the-box music piece consisting of old-school music combined with a new-school beat and feel.

Once the piece is composed, the kids practice and practice for several weeks until it is executed properly by the entire band. To make a long story short, the band uses this piece during competition and wins the tournament, demonstrating that it sometimes pays to think out of the box to achieve the desired success. What they did was get those two styles together, creating a totally unique sound for a band. They brought "new school" and "old school" together for a new sound.

Take practice tests - continuously push yourself through practice tests

Although testing yourself during practice or study sessions should be a normal occurrence, many people don't do it often enough. Constantly testing yourself during your practice, study, or training session is the quickest and most reliable way to determine if you are processing the information. Depending on the activity, there are several ways to test yourself:

- Repeatedly take the chapter review test until you consistently get 90% or better
- Locate subject specific online preparation tests and take until you consistently get 90% or better
- Use the instructor's notes to make the hardest test possible
- Always do the challenge questions at the end of the chapter – don't skip them!
- Use exam simulation programs

When preparing for one of my professional exams, I used the prep-testing method throughout my study session. At first, I tried to create my own mock exams; however, this took too much preparation time. Then I discovered that the certification had several prep-test resources. Some of them were free, and some had a fee attached. However, the prep tests made my studying process much more effective overall.

One time, I had to take a prep exam for several days before I was able to get to 100 percent. First, I started off getting around 65 percent. Then I analyzed the results to understand those areas that needed improvement. Then I practiced and studied until I felt more confident. Then I took the test again and examined my score. I would get up to 75 percent, and then 85 percent, and then 95 percent. Finally, I got up to 100 percent, but I was not satisfied at that point. This was the point when I needed to employ my repetition strategy, so I took the prep test ten more times to make sure I could get 100 percent every time. Once I did that, I was ready to take the actual test, which I passed with flying colors.

For other tests, I have followed the same principles: taking prep tests and going over them again and again until I got 100 percent. And then after I achieved 100 percent, I turned it up a notch and took the test ten times, getting 100 percent each time. To attain optimum performance, you should try this method for basically everything you do: not only for standardized tests but for whatever tests you need to take. Whenever you want to optimally excel on your tests or exams, do a pre-execution test first.

In sports, you can also implement pretests into your practice routine. For example, say that when practicing basketball you are trying to improve your free-throw proficiency. After you have practiced whatever techniques or drills you've been working on, you can test the impact of the free-throw practice session. Depending on what area you are trying to improve, you can set up a test where you will not leave the court until you get a 90 percent on the test. The free-throw test could be anything: for you to make nine out of ten free throws, for example. If two free throws are missed during the test, the test must be started over from the beginning. This test can go on until you make nine out of ten free throws. Similar tests can be used for most sports (golf, tennis, or baseball, for instance) to continuously gauge the practice's effectiveness.

Self-Assessment

Another important area to focus on involves self-assessment, and, specifically, self-observation and self-reflection. Similar to the test-taking process outlined in the previous section, as you practice, you need to continuously be aware of your own performance. You need to focus on correcting and adapting as appropriate. This assessment will allow you to do a self-calibration to help you keep on task for achieving optimum performance.

Metrics and Feedback (Measuring Practice Performance)

The best and most reliable way to improve your practice routine is to measure your progress accurately and consistently. You can accomplish this by using metrics or KPIs (key performance indicators). A common piece of advice for improving performance goes like this: "Measurement is the first step that leads to control and eventually to improvement. If you can't measure something, you can't understand it. If you can't understand it, you can't control it. If you can't control it, you can't improve it." If you don't measure your practice performance, how will you know if you've improved? You can't manage what you don't measure. This is an old management adage that is accurate today. Unless you measure something, you don't know if it is getting better or worse. You can't manage for improvement if you don't measure to see what is getting better and what isn't.

It's not a stretch to say that a person who wishes to perform better or accomplish more needs to have meaningful points of measurement. Here are some examples of practice measurements:

- the ratio of balls versus strikes when a pitcher practices his pitching routine
- various metrics during a practice round of golf including score, fairway drives, greens in regulation, and number of putts
- test scores for practice tests
- how many times a presenter says "uh" during a practice presentation
- average duration of an elevator pitch
- the number of serves in tennis that are put in play

Quite simply, what gets measured gets done. Think about it. The very nature of knowing that something is being monitored causes us to work harder and perform better. When you measure your own practice performance, positive practice results happen:

- You set goals, and evaluate your progress.
- You always know exactly where you stand.

- You identify key aspects you want to refine.
- You see the results of your refinements.
- You quickly and accurately troubleshoot your problems.

You can also measure progress when practicing activities such as a speech or presentation by completing it within a certain time frame, such as twenty minutes. Let's say, for instance, that when practicing the speech, the best time you complete it in is thirty minutes. From this measurement, it is clear that in order to meet the twenty-minute metric, the speech must be trimmed down. In your strategy to reduce the duration of the speech, you would focus on streamlining it by removing some parts and rephrasing or rewriting others until you get the speech down to twenty minutes.

Metrics need to be used for most type of practice methods to help you understand your current progress and make sure you stay on the right track.

Practice Habits

The next area that we'll focus on in the Practice Pillar is practice habits. Mahatma Gandhi said, "An ounce of practice is worth more than tons of preaching." There has been some research done on practice, and one particular study by Professor K. Anders Ericsson at Florida State University (mentioned earlier) found that when practicing, consistency is crucial. Ericsson also notes, "Elite performers in many diverse domains have been found to practice, on the average, roughly the same amount every day, including weekends." Evidence crosses a remarkable range of fields. In building up your habits, it is important to establish a certain comfort level so you can get into your practice and study habits quickly and smoothly, without a lot of obstacles. Here are some suggestions to help you establish a solid practice routine (Ericsson 2006).

Try to Study in the Same Location
Whether you study for business, work, or school, it is more productive to use the same location every time. This might be a certain:

- room in the house
- desk
- area in the office
- section of the library
- favorite coffee shop

Practicing or studying in a familiar location helps maintain your comfort level, and when you are comfortable, you are more likely to have a more effective study session. When practicing sports, it is also advantageous to practice or train in a familiar setting, as you can get into the training session more quickly with less hassle and distractions. For example, when practicing golf, it is helpful to go to a driving range that is familiar so that you can get consistency in your practice. Try to find a range that meets all your needs: close to your home or office, a good price, the flags are in suitable locations, a range that has both mats and grass, a golf pro on location, and so on.

Finally, establishing a familiar location helps your practice succeed because (1) you'll look forward to going to the location, which will motivate you to go more often, and (2) you can set up much more quickly. For example, since I'm so familiar with the setup at Starbucks, I know where the outlets are, and I have already established Wi-Fi connectivity with the standard provider, so I don't need to spend time or worry about plugging in or connecting to the Internet. I already know they have light music playing throughout the shop, so I need to make sure I have my headphones. And I already know that it can get quite chilly there, and I need to bring a light jacket or sweater, just in case. Yep, I live in Starbucks.

Try to Study or Practice at the Same Time

Of course, it is difficult to have consistency in our daily lives. However, if you can establish a consistent study or practice time, this will be beneficial to the overall success of each practice session. Practicing or studying at the same time means you are organizing your overall strategy to incorporate it into your life. It becomes a habitual thing, and you know you need to set aside time to practice each day.

Similar to exercise, if your day gets hectic, you may forget to study or practice. However, if this time is already included in your plans, you'll plan around it (as it's already in your scheduler). Setting this time aside allows you to consistently do the appropriate studying because it's already embedded into your daily life and routine.

Limit Distractions

When you get down to studying and practicing, you want to limit your distractions as best you can. Of course, we will discuss distractions more thoroughly in Pillar Seven (Focus). However, for now we are specifically focusing on limiting distractions during these times of practice or studying.

Practice! Practice!

This is all about practicing, and the important thing is to get your mind ready and set to practice. Famous baseball player, Pete Rose once said, "My father taught me that the only way you can make good at anything is to practice, and then practice some more."

It is interesting that a lot of the stars I've mentioned—Michael Jordan, Jerry Rice, and Tiger Woods—are legendary in their sports fields and have won championships. Jerry Rice has won three Super Bowls, Michael Jordan has won six NBA championships, and Tiger Woods has won fourteen major golf tournaments, so they are legends in their field. They have succeeded, they have been optimal performers, and they *all* stress the need to practice.

Practice is not always the top priority for some athletes, but that type of athlete rarely achieves optimum success.

Studying Techniques

Studying is a subset of practicing and thus quite important. Here are some key pointers for studying. (Note: For more information and guidelines on studying techniques, please go to the Study Guide and Strategies website: http://www. studygs.net/index.htm.)

Make a Study Plan

A study plan is a list of activities you plan to do to prepare for an exam. A few days before the exam, take the time to write out a study plan on a simple sheet of notepaper.

Your first task will be to confirm the date and time of the exam. Then create the plan according to the priorities in your life (i.e., your job, family, classes, and so on). Next, determine the study or practice methods you will use: flash cards, deliberate studying, memorization, or target notes. Make studying efficient, and don't have a lot of loose ends or overhead to deal with when it's time to study. Get to the point so you are studying the things that the instructor, coach, or boss wants you to learn—not studying to just study, but to accomplish your goal. If your goal is just to learn, then study to learn, of course. But use your time wisely and efficiently so that you cover the items that will be on the test.

To study efficiently, you need to quickly determine what items are the highest priorities. Those top priority items are usually the most highly ranked, most highly weighted, or have the most impact. Focus on those impacting items first, as top priority items usually make up the majority of exams.

When you study, get an overall perspective of the subject matter to determine what to study. Sometimes it is difficult to study in a vacuum, so examine the subject-matter scope. Do a high-level walk-through of the entire topic to get a sense of things. For instance, if you are reading a book, quickly skim through the chapters and get an initial feel of the subject matter.

Understand the current status of your study situation. For example, do you have two weeks to study, or is the test tomorrow? Do you have a lot of study material to get through (the book, study notes, and study guide), or do you have minimal information and need to contact your peers to get more? Will life pressures such as a busy work schedule, chaotic family life, or other exams in the same period impact your situation? Knowing the situation will enable you to adjust your study plan accordingly.

Also, if there are certain topics that cause you some grief, make sure that you address these areas quickly and thoroughly. It helps to attack the key areas that you are struggling and weak in first. Try not to shy away from those subjects, but, rather, meet them head on, because if you don't, they will definitely hurt you during the test.

Below is a list of activities that may be included on a study plan:

1. Make a study guide that contains the key ideas.
2. Establish a consistent time of day to study.
3. Establish the duration intervals of study time (i.e., studying two hours at a time).
4. Determine the subject matter (i.e., math, history, or English).
5. Confirm your study goals (determine that you want to be at a specific point at a certain time).
6. Establish the study technique.
7. Write down questions regarding things you are unclear about.
8. Get those questions answered by instructors, tutors, and/or classmates.
9. Write up solutions to types of questions you expect to see on the exam.
10. Practice homework problems.
11. Study with a friend.

When Studying Is Not Working
If your approach to studying is not effective—meaning you are not getting the subject matter or it's not penetrating your brain—then perhaps you need to get a

better handle on the subject matter. Maybe this is a sign that you don't know the subject well enough, and you should go back, and reread the section of book that you are struggling with, or review the notes again.

If you try this and still continue to struggle, then it is time to utilize some of the suggestions from Pillar Three (Knowledge) and seek expert help or consultation from a tutor, instructor, coach, or trainer. Be sure to address those struggles first before moving on. If you don't thoroughly understand something completely, then you are not progressing effectively, and you are simply wasting time at that point. Therefore, it's important that you go back to Pillar Three, and pick out one of those strategies that can help close the gap and mitigate your struggles.

Shortcuts

I am, in general, against using shortcuts to accomplish activities, but in some cases, when efficient shortcuts are utilized, it's not only acceptable, but encouraged, to use them, as they provide a speedier method for studying. The main objective is to get the most out of studying in an efficient and productive manner. There are ways that you can be more efficient, such as using formulas in math or using a calculator. I often use acronyms as shortcuts for certain types of vocabulary words or certain phrases. Another shortcut method is developing mental drills that allow you to remember difficult items more easily. These are just some of the good, legitimate, and efficient types of shortcuts that will help you memorize and get through some of the more difficult, hard-to-absorb topics.

Studying Outside the Box

As mentioned earlier, utilizing outside-the-box techniques is a good way to introduce new thinking into your normal routine or process. If your studying sessions aren't as productive as you hoped, try to do new things—try different study techniques and drills. Go outside the box while staying within the boundaries of your studying. This means that if you normally use flash cards to study but have never used prep tests, then perhaps it's time to give prep tests a try to see if this method might work for you. If you are a book studier, maybe it's time to look at some of the notes from the teacher instead of just relying on the book. You'll find that each method can complement the other in some way. Sometimes you need to get out of your comfort zone and use other studying techniques that you normally don't use.

Taking Breaks

When practicing, studying, and/or training, it's important to know when and how to take breaks. Yes, breaks! It is important to take breaks, as they enable you to recharge, refresh, and get your mind back on point. If you study continuously for hours on end without a break, you can start to burn out and end up making excuses not to study anymore, which may cause you to end the session earlier than planned. In that situation, you still end up taking a break, but, unfortunately, it comes at the expense of valuable study time.

Timing Out Your Breaks

Therefore, you need to learn how to take breaks, when to take them, and what optimal break frequency is. As for how to take breaks, this is totally up to you and what works for you. There is no rule of thumb to adhere to. However, many people (me included) like to use a four to one study-to-break ratio. This means that for every four units (e.g., minutes) of study time, you should incorporate one unit of break time.

Suggested: EPOP Break Time Guidelines	
Study Time (minutes)	Break Time (minutes)
60	15
80	20
120	30

For example, if you are studying math, you might go real hard for an hour, and then take a fifteen-minute break. Or if you want to go two straight hours, then you would need a thirty-minute break. If you need to take more than thirty minutes for break time, then you should conclude your study session, and restart the session when you are ready. How and when you take breaks depends on what works well for you. Once you have a set pattern in place, try to stick with that pattern.

It is important to establish and declare your study/break pattern before each session to avoid taking impromptu, unscheduled, and unorganized breaks. Having an established break pattern allows you take more consistent and effective breaks, and, therefore, use your time more wisely.

A great strategy is to use a timer to control and organize your study/break sessions. For example, before you start studying, set your timer to sixty minutes, and then stick to studying the entire sixty minutes. Don't leave the study area and don't stop studying until the timer goes off. When the timer alarm goes off, set the timer to fifteen minutes, and then take your break.

Organizing Your Breaks

What you do during your break is entirely up to you. However, first you should do the things that would normally interrupt your study time, such as going to the restroom; getting something to eat; having a smoke; following up on phone calls, texts, and e-mails; or catching up on the news for a quick snapshot of what's going on in the world. During my break periods, I'm addicted to turning on ESPN to see what's going on in the sports world. My son seems to think that you do all those things first once the break timer goes off. For example, when his study timer goes off, he sets it to fifteen minutes, and then he usually goes and watches TV for the duration of the timer break. Then once the timer goes off again, he goes to the restroom, gets something to eat, and so on. *Wrong!* Everything should be taken care of during the timer break. Once the break timer goes off, it's time to go back to studying.

Another break activity I enjoy is going outside and breathing in the fresh air. I enjoy listening to the birds chirping and playing or watching them fly. I relish the small things, such as seeing if it's raining or sunny outside. To me, it's important to get back in touch with the outside world. Otherwise, when I'm studying, especially if I'm studying hard, I get distracted and wonder, *What's going on in the world? What's out there?* If I don't get outside, I usually feel kind of isolated. So it is important for me to get out there and take it all in.

Setting up Break Milestones

Depending on the type of activity you are engaged in, there are different types of break thresholds you can set to keep your study, practice, or training and break session organized. Here are some ideas:

- Studying: Take fifteen minutes for every sixty minutes of study.
- Golf: Take a ten-minute break after hitting a hundred golf balls
- Basketball: Take fifteen minutes after shooting fifty free throws.
- Exercising: Take fifteen minutes after sixty minutes of intense exercise.
- Reading: Take twenty minutes after reading fifty pages.

These are just some examples of how you can set up break sessions for the activities in your life. Identify what works for you, and then stick with it.

Practice Pillar Final Thoughts

An important step in going from good to great is understanding and accepting that it is OK to keep learning, growing, and improving. It is a positive strategy to pick up training, coaching, tutoring, and education where necessary.

However, this chapter revealed that after attaining the appropriate knowledge, the next step is to thoroughly and exhaustively practice this knowledge as well as the areas you already know well. In order to achieve greatness, an intense and frequent practice strategy must be employed.

The next chapter, Communication Pillar, will show how communication, when used appropriately, is the key and glue to pulling all the pillars together for maximum, efficiency, effectiveness, and optimum success.

CHAPTER 9

Know Who's on First...

Pillar Five: Communication

n a typical workday, I have several communication activities. I start my day by communicating with God through prayer and by reading the Bible. Then I communicate with my family before we all go our separate ways to work, school, and so on.

As I drive to the office, I often communicate to the other commuters on the highways of Los Angeles, particularly on the I-405, as I inform them of their challenging driving skills and habits via the horn of my car. Unfortunately, they often communicate back to me the same way.

Also on my hour-long commute, my cell phone is hard at work as I often communicate with colleagues over the phone as well as participate in meetings. And sometimes, when the car is not moving due to traffic, I send text messages and e-mails over the phone and read incoming e-mail as well.

Since I am a "coffee snob," I often stop at the nearest Starbucks, and I have a little small talk with the Starbucks barista and with other loyal Starbucks coffee drinkers. And since I am a loyal and frequent Starbucks patron, I pay for my coffee using a communication payment application on my iPhone, as I never use cash there anymore.

When I finally make it to the office building, I often run into fellow employees and chat with them. I usually say hello or have a brief conversation with the company receptionist before going upstairs to my office. In my office, I have a wireless laptop computer and an iPad. My computer screen is filled with several lines of e-mail ready to be read. I have several computer windows open for instant messaging (IM) chats with colleagues around the world using Microsoft Lync. My smartphones also have both work and personal e-mails, along with texting capabilities.

As I sit down ready to start my day, I get an alert from e-mail, IM, and text sent by my calendar application from all four devices informing me that I have an important meeting in fifteen minutes via video conferencing. For my meeting, I start up an audio conferencing bridge, where hundreds of people can be on the bridge simultaneously. In addition to the audio bridge, I also open up a web-conferencing session, which allows the meeting participants to view the presenter's desktop as the presenter shares the presentation across the globe. If that isn't enough communication, we can also visually see the main presenters via video conferencing. Therefore, my colleagues and I will have a productive global meeting communicating via audio, web, and video.

This is just a small sample of the power of communication and the tools we can access that enable us to communicate more effectively, efficiently, and productively. Communication is the pillar that ties all the pillars together. It is the glue pillar.

As the example above clearly shows, we communicate with others for the better part of our daily activities. Whether in a meeting, on the phone, via text message, during a presentation, through a memo, or one-on-one, we interface with people.

What Is Communication About?

Communication is about getting clear, concise, and effective information in the most efficient and productive manner to the people who will help you succeed in achieving your goal. It's also about those people providing constructive and timely feedback to help you optimally perform.

Within EPOP™, communication is anything that allows people to interface with one another. It also refers to the interchange of thoughts and ideas with the aim of handing over information. The Communication Pillar's scope entails several different types of interfaces:

- one-on-one
- team or group communication
- communication tools
- written
- oral
- presentation

Whether through meetings, presentations, speeches, phone, fax, e-mails, memos, Internet, smartphones, or social networking sites (such as Facebook and Twitter), you need to communicate to perform at any level, not to mention at the optimum level. There are many ways to deliver communication to others. The ability to effectively communicate your thoughts, ideas, plans, and strategies is important, and it is usually underrated and overlooked.

Communication Tools and Communication Management

Communication tools can include productivity tools (such as word-processing tools), presentation tools, spreadsheets, project management tools, and smartphone applications. However, communication is about more than just tools; it is about managing your performance to get the optimum success. You are, in a sense, the project manager of your performance. To be successful, you need to ensure your progress by keeping in constant communication with whatever parties impact your success. For example, if you're not performing up to your abilities in the classroom, it is up to you to communicate your challenges to your professor, other classmates, and tutors so they can help you get the resources you need to be more successful. If you are struggling, how will anyone know, unless you communicate that to them? If you don't communicate this, no one will be able to help.

Essentially, in order to be successful in achieving optimum performance, you must be the administrator of your entire EPOP™ strategy, and in order to be a successful administrator in anything, you must be able to communicate clearly and effectively. It is your responsibility to manage all communication. It is your responsibility to be proactive and anticipate what you need to be successful. You need to focus on making things happen because activities will not move forward, tasks will not get done, and progress will not be made unless you drive things forward and make them happen.

Communication Phases within EPOP™

For each activity, there are three primary phases of communication within EPOP™:

1. Before performing the activity
2. During the activity
3. After performing the activity

Communication before Performing the Activity

The first phase of communication involves all the communication events leading up to the execution of the actual activity. This phase contains everything that happens before you actually go "onstage" (wherever you actually perform the activity). This phase involves the coordination and planning, where you need to communicate to the participants, colleagues, and stakeholders the status and plans for your upcoming activity.

Recruit Your Cheerleaders

This is also a good time to recruit or involve supporters and allies in your communication strategy. Reach out to people who will support you, cheer you on, and keep you going through your pre-execution phase. These people can then be there when you actually execute your activity. For example, if you are participating in a sporting event such as a softball game, and you need support for the game, you need to communicate in a timely manner the logistics (date, time, and location) of the event so the supporters can attend. Similarly, if you have a presentation, speech, or music recital coming up, communicating effectively will enhance the likelihood of getting the support you desire on the big day.

Normally, those people who are your cheerleaders are people relatively close to you, like your spouse, kids, parents, siblings, coworkers, and anybody in your circle who usually cheers you on. You want to engage this support group early and communicate what you are trying to achieve. With this support strategy, you can let them know if you need or want help in achieving your goals.

Build Your Support Groups

You can also get involved with support groups through social-network tools such as Facebook, LinkedIn, and Twitter. For instance, when you join a weight-loss program, part of that program usually entails participating in support groups through online forums, blogs, newsletters, seminars, and conference calls. These types of online support are helpful because the participants in these groups have gone through, or are going through, a similar situation. As you communicate your story online, the group can offer advice, tips, motivation, inspiration, and encouragement. For example, if your goal is to lose weight, there are many weight-loss forums online to help you get motivated and stay motivated so you can continue to succeed. As you continue to communicate your weight-loss journey, the group will be there through your ups and downs. Research shows that these types of motivational support groups are highly successful.

Suppose that, as an aspiring runner, you seek to run in an upcoming 5K or even a marathon. One way to help you achieve this goal is to participate in an online runners' support group, such as Runner's World's forum (which is a forum with news, information, and advice for runners, offering everything from running equipment reviews to training techniques for races and marathons). These forums have information for beginners to marathoners on everything from equipment and apparel to upcoming events. Online communication forums also typically feature areas for discussion, FAQs, running jargon, running book and movie reviews, and more.

By joining support groups such as these, you can reap the benefits of online cheering as the support group keeps you going and inspires you to try harder next time. There are all kinds of motivating factors offered through these support groups, and they can often give you the extra inspiration and motivation you need to continue on. This is a valuable example of how communication can help you reach your optimum best.

Status Checking

Another key component of communication prior to an activity involves continually checking the status of the activity's progress. Depending on the type of activity, you can check the status via meetings, e-mails, phone calls, and texts to get updates from various sources, including work colleagues, business partners, coaches, trainers, tutors, teachers, the event venue, and vendors.

Managing the status is crucial to the ultimate success of your activity. You will be able to determine if you are on course or on target toward achieving your goal. For instance, through status checking you can get valuable feedback and input from relevant sources that will help determine the activity's progress in certain areas at that point. From this input, you can make adjustments to your plan and strategy as needed to help you get back on task. The most effective approach to monitoring and managing your status is through communication.

Identifying Issues and Red Flags

Another important component of communicating effectively prior to the actual activity or event involves identifying issues and red flags quickly and efficiently. Once these issues are identified, it is important to address and fix them or to communicate clearly to the person causing the issue to ensure it is resolved on that end. Communicating issues to interested and relevant parties is important, as these trusted individuals can generally help resolve them more quickly. But they can't help if you don't communicate.

Corporate and Business Communications

Communication problems in the workplace can cost your company or business productivity and money. Without efficient communication, your company will be challenged in exchanging information that is critical to daily operations. Understanding examples of corporate and business communication issues can help you create policies that will address problems and set up an efficient communication environment in the workplace.

One-way communication is an example of how communication can be ineffective across a company. For example, most companies send out either impromptu or periodic company-wide broadcasts in hopes of communicating relevant information to their employees. However, sometimes these communications contain information or news that is not interesting to a majority of the audience, so they disregard them. In addition, the communication may be unorganized and difficult to read, or may be presented in a format that's not concise and quickly readable. A department that sends out information in a confusing format needs to be informed immediately, or the information from that group will always pose a challenge.

It's important to ensure that there is a way to communicate these challenges back to the senders. Employees and leadership staff should be able to provide feedback at all times to improve the quality of information being disseminated and the manner in which it is delivered.

Communication during the Activity (When It Counts)

It's one thing to ensure you adequately prepare for your activity through solid and efficient communication; however, it's another to communicate optimally when it counts and when it is truly execution time. When you participate in an activity where you must communicate—such as a speech, presentation, sales pitch, writing an article, teaching, or coaching—then in order to successfully execute the activity, you must ensure that you have mastered the fundamentals of communication: oral, written, presentation, and even nonverbal.

In order to communicate flawlessly, you need to ensure that your environment is properly set up and aligned for your success. For example, if you are doing a presentation, before you even get up to the stage you want to make sure that everything is loaded on the computer properly. You want to check that the sound is adequate, and the microphone is working. You need to have your environment right so you have the opportunity to succeed. There's nothing worse than not being able to hear a presenter on the stage because the mic isn't working properly.

If used the right way, communication techniques can positively influence an activity's ultimate results. For example, in football, in order to move the football down the field, the offense must run different plays against the defense. If the correct plays are called, and the offense continues to advance the ball until it scores, then the offense is successful. However, the key to scoring in football is for the offense to run plays that take advantage of a defense's weakness on a given play. In order to run offensive plays, the quarterback must get the play from the coach.

The traditional method of communicating a play from the coach to the quarterback is by sending the play via another player. This means that after a play is completed, the coach tells one of his players the play from the sideline, and then that player runs on the field to replace another player and communicate the play to the quarterback. The quarterback gathers up the offense and repeats the play to the entire offensive team.

Whether they are playing Pop Warner, high school, college, or the NFL, most football teams today use this traditional method to communicate plays to the players in the huddle. A huddle is a gathering of the offensive team in a close circle or line behind the line of scrimmage for instructions, signals, etc., from the team captain or quarterback, usually held before each offensive play. The huddle is used to effectively communicate to the team on the football field. However, some high-school and college teams use more complex methods to communicate plays to get a greater edge on the defense. These teams are using a "no-huddle" offense, which means that after the offense runs a football play, they don't go into the huddle to communicate, but instead the team communicates with each other through secret signals transmitted from the coach on the sideline.

The communication challenge to the no-huddle offense is how to get plays to the players without huddling. Several methods are used. Some teams use a code that is a combination of words or commands that are either real or fake, and then combine those signals with numbers.

Other methods include hand signals, wristbands, and code words. However, one of the most successful communication systems belongs to the Oregon Ducks football team. Oregon, one of the most productive, furious-paced offenses in the nation in 2014, uses images to relay the play call from the sideline. It is their philosophy that using pictures is much quicker and more efficient than hand signals. In 2014, the Ducks went no-huddle almost exclusively. They spent as little as thirteen seconds between plays and didn't give the defense time to make substitutions or adjustments. Their basic strategy relied on not giving defenders time to think or breathe. With this offensive scheme, they've outscored bewildered opponents by a ratio of four to one after halftime during the season.

The Oregon Ducks use a unique and reliable image-based signaling system that takes about five to ten seconds to process and run a play. They typically use six signal boards during games, each featuring four images. To opposing coaches and players, the images on the boards appear completely random and, frankly, a little outrageous. One placard used in a game, for instance, had the word "magic" spelled out, a photograph of an animal, the outline of the state of Oregon, and a picture of a famous TV sports announcer. On average, the Ducks used the placards to call about 25 percent of their plays, enabling them to hike the ball so quickly after the previous play that it was nearly impossible for defenses to make substitutions.

Oregon's complicated communication system is a prime example of using communication to enhance the execution of your core activity or service. However, communication strategies do not have to be complex and exhaustive to be effective; they simply have to be clearly understood by the impacted parties. For instance, simply communicating the accurate time, date, location, subject matter, and agenda of a meeting will help the meeting run smoother than if any one of those items was not communicated to all parties.

Communication after the Activity Is Finished (Now What?)

After you've completed the activity, it is important to use communication techniques to identify the results of the activity and to capture any information that can help you improve your success in the next opportunity. Depending on the activity, there are several methods used to capture results. Here are a couple of methods, to name just a few:

- send a follow-up letter or e-mail after an interview
- surveys
- examine before and after sales

- word of mouth
- applause
- blog responses
- increased registrations
- increased website hits
- Facebook likes
- stats
- measurements
- scores

If you go on a job interview, sending a follow-up letter to the interviewer afterward is always a good idea. Likewise, if you gave a presentation and you need to know if the presentation was effective, the audience can provide communication feedback in several ways. They can provide immediate positive feedback through applause, laughter, constant eye contact, interactive participation, and questions, or just as easily provide negative communication via silence, blank stares, not paying attention, and not asking any questions.

Feedback can also be retrieved by gathering data after the presentation or speech is over. For instance, quick and simple surveys can be taken from the audience to gauge their immediate thoughts about the presentation. Here are a set of sample survey questions:

1. Please rate the presentation from one to ten.
2. What was the main take-away from the presentation?
3. What did you like the most?
4. What did you like the least?
5. Are you interested in receiving more information regarding this topic?

You get the picture. Try to quickly get a sense of what the audience thought about the presentation so you can determine its effectiveness. With survey data, you can closely analyze the information and develop customized queries and reports to identify strong areas in the presentation and areas that need improvement.

Another measurement that communicates your performance is sales. At the end of speeches, presenters often position themselves outside the exits of the venues with tables or booths set up to sell books, CDs, DVDs, and tickets to future events. The sale and buzz of these items is often an indicator of whether you had a compelling and successful performance or not. If at the end of your presentation, people are lined up for several minutes to buy your promotional material, then that is a pretty good indicator that you have effectively communicated to your audience. However, if nobody stops to purchase your material, perhaps the information was not as compelling as you would like to think, and you may need to make adjustments to your presentation.

Winning Communication Hints and Tips

Here are some key communication points that are useful for all types of communication: written, oral, and formal presentations. They should be used as guidelines. Following these tips will help you succeed in achieving your optimum performance in your targeted activity.

Summarize, Explain, and Close

Always provide a summary or an overview when you start communicating with someone. First, summarize what the subject matter is about. The mistake many people make is that they jump directly "deep into the weeds" and into the details and start explaining without any frame of reference or context.

I heard this saying some time ago. I'm not sure where or from whom, but it has stuck with me ever since. In order to properly communicate:

Tell them what you are going to tell them...
Tell them,
Then tell them what you told them.

I coined this phrase: the EPOP™ "Tell Them" Sandwich.

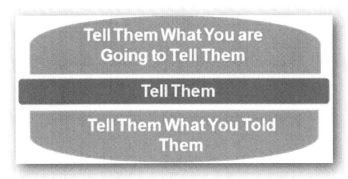

Copyright © 2015 Ainiare Enterprises

Basically, I've enhanced the "Tell Them" sandwich so that I can use it in nearly every communication project, whether it is a blog, article, book, term paper, speech, presentation, or sales pitch.

First, in the "Tell Them What You Are Going to Tell Them" sandwich section, you need to summarize or "level set" with the audience to ensure that everyone is on the same page. Start with a light and brief overview, and then dig into the next points that are relevant to the task at hand. In the summary, provide a high-level view, or overview, of the subject matter and a frame of reference so that the audience understands what the subject is about as you prepare them for the details that lie ahead.

Next, in the "Tell Them" sandwich section, the focus is on explaining the relevant details about the items communicated in the summary. This sandwich section should be the largest.

Finally, in the "Tell Them What You Told Them" sandwich section, wrap things up by summarizing again what you told them to ensure they understood the details correctly.

Here's an example of a brief "Tell Them" sandwich in article format:

Baldwin Hills: On Thursday, August 22, 2009, the Universe High School Tigers freshman football team served notice that this is a new year with a new winning attitude as they delivered a rousing and decisive victory over Carson High School 41–0. The Tigers used an aggressive big-play running attack, an explosive passing attack, and a stingy and bruising defense to overwhelm the Carson team.

Universe used an effective running combination of Jack Teramo (#2), Jose Gough (#5), and Michael Harman (#8) to mount up impressive rushing yards, while Harman executed an efficient passing game to near perfection as he passed for 5–8, 121 yards, 3 TDs, and 0 ints.

After receiving the opening kickoff, Universe quickly drove the ball down the field for the first score. Teramo had a 12-yard run, and then Harman had a couple of 1st-down runs of 10 and 20 yards before connecting with Joe Hobbs (#44) for a 12-yard TD pass.

On the next play from scrimmage, Carson fumbled the ball at the 50-yard line, and the Tigers' offense was back in business. However, after a couple good runs by Teramo and Harman, the drive stalled at the 20-yard line after Harman was slammed to the ground. He had to sit out for the remaining plays of the series until he was able to fully recover from the hit. The Tigers tried for a 37-yard field goal, but it was unsuccessful.

After Carson's offense was stopped again after only 3 plays, the Tigers offense started on Carson's 35 yard line. On the first play of the drive, Teramo swept to the left side and punished 3 defenders before exploding into the end zone for an exciting 35-yard TD.

The Tiger's next drive started on Carson's 30-yard line after another defensive stop by the Tigers. It took only 2 plays for the Tigers to get into the end zone again. Teramo had a bruising 20-yard run, and then Gough (#5) swept around the left side, and like a beast he "trucked" a would-be defender before doing a Superman dive into the end zone for a 10-yard TD.

Just before the 1st half ended, the Tiger's passing attack went into high gear after another quick stop by the defense. From Universe's 25-yard line, Harman threw a 25-yard pass to Christian Anthony (#4) and a 10-yard pass to Victor Shelton (#10) before connecting with Hobbs for a 44-yard bomb TD with only 35 seconds left in the half. The half ended with Universe leading 27–0.

In the second half, the Universe offense used a 30-yard TD pass to Anthony and 5-yard drive by Arnold Eves (#33) to finish the scoring. But the other story of the game was the Universe defense, as it continued its pounding, relentless, penetrating, stingy attack by shutting down the Carson offense. The tough defense was led by Jon Jacobs (#41), Hobbs, and Steve Collose (#9).

It was a great win for the program to help start on a positive note. The team had tremendous support from parents, family members, and fellow students. Universe will try to improve its record to 2–0 next week as they travel to Pitterson Hills High School on Thursday, September 30 at 3:15 p.m.

Know Your Audience

In all forms of communication—whether verbal, written, or presentation—it is imperative that you know your audience. This means knowing who wants to hear you or what you are attempting to communicate so that they can support you in some fashion.

Imagine doing a speech on global warming where you are speaking to the folks at a hot-rod convention (where things such as global warming may not be high on their agenda). Most likely, your speech will not be as warmly welcomed as you would have hoped. So make sure you know the audience you are trying to reach. This will provide you with a better chance to succeed in communicating with your target.

Be Efficient

Being efficient involves achieving maximum productivity with minimum wasted effort or expense. In communication, it's important to get to your audience as quickly and efficiently as possible. In today's competitive global environment, the ability to efficiently communicate is imperative to being an optimal performer.

The key ingredient in efficient communication is brevity. Communication must be time limited, decisive, and meaningful. You want to be efficient and concise in whatever communication forum you enter. It is not efficient to use a bunch of big words or a lot of words to try to show people how smart you are; you want to get to the point and make it as concise and short as possible so that you can continue to captivate their attention. Be as direct as possible within the boundaries of good manners. Avoiding the point confuses people and makes them lose interest in what you're saying.

Be Positive

Always communicate from a positive point of view. It's important to keep the tone positive, as this helps keep people willing to listen to what you have to say and prevents them from feeling defensive. Whatever type of communication you use, always remember etiquette. Being courteous is a much better way to put a person at ease than being rude. Someone who feels open and at ease is much more likely to be receptive to what you have to say.

People do not respond well to negative communication. Even though you might need to convey something unpleasant, you can still be positive when you explain it.

Respect the Receiver

One of the key principles of successful communication is to respect the receivers of your information. Respect their time, their intelligence, and the fact that they are making an effort to read your material or listen to your presentation. Respect what they are doing, and don't just think you are better than they are and assume they will listen regardless.

When someone calls my house and, without a proper introduction, simply says, "Let me speak to so-and-so" or "Is your wife home?" that person is acting as if I'm not there or don't matter. So I usually say, "May I ask who's calling?" However, I shouldn't have to, because when you call, e-mail, or text someone, it is respectful to introduce yourself. The source needs to be clearly identified. Whether it's in your e-mail signature, your text message, your documents, or your presentation, the source of the communication and the contact information needs to be clearly acknowledged. In short, respect the receiver, and you will have more success.

Be Reachable

Fortunately (or unfortunately, depending on how you look at it), I am reachable in numerous ways. I have two cell phones (voice, text, e-mail, voice mail), one home phone (voice-only, voice mail), several e-mail accounts, Facebook and Twitter accounts, and websites. Oh, and I can also be reached in person. In order for you to be successful, people need to be able to contact you when necessary. Therefore, it is important that you make sure you can be reached. Of course, you don't need to be available to everyone; however, if you are building and maintaining key relationships, those contacts need to be able to get a hold of you.

Be reachable in person, if possible. If not, be reachable with an e-mail or make sure people can call you and leave a voice mail. If you are not available, sign up for an answering service.

Likewise, ensure you make your contact information available and accessible to potential partners, clients, and business relations. It is extremely frustrating when you see something you may be interested in pursuing, but the source leaves minimal or outdated contact information. There may be a name but no number, no e-mail, and no clear way to contact the source. So ensure that you not only provide contact information but that you are reachable and available through that contact information.

Follow the "Golden Rule" of Communication

We all know the Golden Rule: "Do unto others as you would have them do unto you," In communication, think about how you would like to receive a message.

You want to be treated with respect and in a positive manner. You want people to respond to you in a timely fashion. Therefore, provide that same respect and positive energy every time you communicate, and you will usually get the desired response.

More "Sometimes" Is Better

Earlier I said to be concise, so this statement might seem conflicting. However, more is better than less, meaning that you can be concise, but, at the same time, you need to provide as much detail as possible to ensure that people have the appropriate information. For example, say you want people to join you for lunch and a basketball game at the Staples Center. What if you sent the following e-mail message? "You are invited to a wonderful event at the Staples Center. Please join us. Jeff." The message is concise, which is OK, but much of the relevant information is left out. Therefore, more is needed: specifically, information such as when this is will happen, the cost of this event, whether parking is available, the location and address, directions, and so on.

When you put any communication together give your audience all the information they need to be able to act on it. To make sure you are providing clearer instructions and communication, more is usually better when used in a concise manner.

Communication Tools

Whenever possible, use communication tools such as smartphones, tablets, and computers. They are absolute necessities in today's world. Use these tools to run applications such as Microsoft Office, mobile apps, texting, e-mail, Twitter, Facebook, Internet browsing, and much more. Use as many tools as possible to make things more efficient for you.

Humor

Incorporate humor whenever appropriate and whenever possible. Humor is the best way to lighten the mood and show the audience a different side of you. Whenever there is an opportunity to inject humor, do so. Good and appropriate humor goes a long way in effective communication.

No Questions Allowed

When I initiate communication via an e-mail, status report, memo, presentation, or sales pitch, I always have an internal competition with myself to see how few questions I get back from the audience. If I do not get any questions back, I consider it a successfully sent communication. If I get a couple of questions, then I look at them and work on how to improve the next time. If I get a lot of questions and requests for clarifications, I do not give myself a good grade on my delivery, and I look to make drastic improvements on my communication the next time around.

It is imperative that you ensure your communication answers all possible questions the audience may have. Many times you have only one shot at capturing your audience, and they will quickly become unsure or disinterested if they have unanswered questions.

For instance, before sending an e-mail memo, read it over, ask yourself questions, and see if that memo has answered those questions. If the memo answers all your possible questions, then send it. Your goal should be that no one will ask a clarifying question after receiving information from you and that all bases have been covered. Of course, there are always wayward questions that you didn't think of, but the point is to think of as many as you can, and try to make sure you have addressed everything.

Know the Requirements and Boundaries

Understand the activity's requirements, directions, rules, and guidelines ahead of time so that you are able to respond accordingly. You will need to clearly disseminate these to key stakeholders.

For example, in a previous job I worked on bids and proposals. Many of the bids and proposals that we submitted were far from what the customers wanted or required. We included extra things that we thought the customers should have; however, we needed to understand that we were not thoroughly considering the requirements the customers had given us. Instead, we provided what we thought they really wanted. We didn't win a lot of bids because we didn't pay attention to the requirements. In some cases, when you do not get the proper requirements, you miss the goal entirely.

When I first started my career, I was a young buck out of college. I was given a project to do: a mock-up of a full-scale satellite to display to defense customers at a major show. Although I was a young man out engineering school, I had no idea how a satellite worked, let alone how to do a mock-up. Nevertheless, I requested all the requirements and got all the directions, rules, guidelines, specifications from the experienced engineers. I needed to understand several elements, such as what the specifications were of the real satellite, who the audience was, why they wanted to see this, what the reason for it was, whether there were examples of similar mock-ups that were done before, and so on.

After I gathered all that information and spent time with different people going over the requirements, directions, drawings, guidelines, and specifications, I made sure I stayed within what my boss was looking for and what the customer required. This turned out to be one of the best projects I have ever done in my career. The customer was satisfied as well. But the key was making sure that I understood, analyzed, and followed the project requirements.

The point is, try to thoroughly understand what is expected and required. Read the requirements, directions, rules, and guidelines so that you can come as close as possible to presenting what the customer wants.

Provide Accurate Information

It should go without saying that you need to make sure you provide accurate information in all your communications (e-mails, memos, speeches, and presentations). Check and double-check your information before communicating, because inaccurate information can ruin your credibility. If your information is publicly challenged and it's proven to be incorrect, then the audience will question the validity of all the information in the document or speech. So make sure you provide accurate information in whatever you do and whenever you communicate.

Delegate

Communication is important in delegating tasks. The way you communicate to individuals and the way you delegate the particular task should be handled with care and respect in order to get the most out of them. When you delegate a specific task, do it in an organized, well-thought-out, well-planned manner. When you delegate the task in a way that is efficient and fair, and communicate what you are doing, the individual will be empowered and want to complete the task for you.

Be a Soldier Sometimes

Sometimes it is a challenge for people, especially people in leadership roles, to take orders from someone else. It's difficult to be a soldier when you're usually a general. However, in some cases you may be in situations where you need to follow orders instead of giving them (e.g., a new project, tiger team, new role, or new company). Therefore, it is important to understand how to communicate in those situations.

It is important to understand and identify what your goals are and what you plan to achieve. Work through this, learn something from it, and do not respond in a negative manner whatsoever. Treat whoever is giving the orders with respect, and then do what you need to do to fulfill your overall goal.

Shut Up, and Listen!

Sometimes we need to simply shut up and listen. People sometimes talk too much. They want to get their words out; they want to be heard. They want people to think they are smart. Sometimes, the best thing to do is to shut up and listen, and then let somebody else talk. Absorb the information that is provided to you, and speak when it is appropriate.

When you try to "hog" the floor, people can interpret this as being rude and disrespectful. When that occurs, you can turn people off, and then what you are trying to convey will become tainted and not get the impact it deserves—all because you did not listen to them first. The more intimately you listen to others, the more successful you will be in communicating your thoughts to them according to their frames of reference. By listening to others, you will know how they think, what their desired expectations are, and how you can stimulate their curiosity and get their attention.

Keep Everyone in the Loop

It's always important to keep key stakeholders in the loop. Even if they do not have apparent, active roles in the current project, you should make them aware of what's going on, as their areas may be impacted. When we communicate, we often communicate only to the front-office and customer-facing people (i.e., sales, marketing, business development, and management) but forget about the back-office people (i.e., service, processing, facilities, operations, logistics, IT systems group, audio visual, and food preparation). However, these areas can sometimes make or break your event or activity.

Make it a point to keep everyone included in the overall relevant news, as all team members play roles in the activity's success.

Be Transparent

Know how to communicate your fears, challenges, and current issues so that problems can be promptly addressed. There are many times when people have challenges or problems, but they do not communicate them because they are afraid others will see them as problem starters or problem makers, or assume that they cannot solve problems themselves.

However, if you communicate issues, challenges, and problems in an organized, coherent, and uncomplaining fashion, more people will accept them and work with you to solve them. More often than not, you will find out that many people had the same issues you did but were afraid to express them or were not comfortable doing so.

Have Thick Skin

Be able to accept criticism and feedback in order to get better. This is a key aspect of communicating: you need to have a mind-set that maybe some of what you put out there is not quite agreeable to other people. Or they may not see the same situation as you do. These people may criticize you and offer feedback or opinions. They may not even like you and might talk about you. However, you need to be above it all and not get defensive. Listen to the feedback, and go back, and reevaluate your information to see what criticisms have merit and validity. Then make the appropriate changes and issue another version.

Never avoid taking criticism or feedback. You have to get out of the mind-set that everything you do is perfect, because it's not. You are not perfect. What you are trying to be is the best you can be. Your focus should always be directed toward getting better at whatever you do.

Proactive Communication

In proactive communication, instead of waiting for something to happen, you lead the charge and make the first move in the given situation. Sometimes this involves little things, such as speaking up and informing your boss that you want to advance in your career or that you want more responsibility to be promoted.

Communicating proactively simply means that you are communicating your goals and needs to people who can help you reach them, instead of just sitting back and waiting for them to come to you. It's about speaking up for what you believe in and want to have happen with your life. If you've ever heard the phrase "the squeaky wheel gets the grease," then you will understand that you need to be the squeaky wheel. Since opportunities don't often fall in your lap, you need to be proactive and lead them to you.

For example, again in my early years at TRW, I was identified as being one of the high potential achievers for the future, along with about five other young people. We were called "High Pots." One of the benefits of being High Pots was that we got to participate in high-level discussions with senior management. This exposure gave us some visibility and the opportunity to feel what being an executive is like. One time, there was a round-table session at one of the vice president's lunches (they called these sessions "Brown Bags"). The vice president asked everybody what they wanted to do in five years, ten years. The query went around the room to each of the High Pots, and each one had fairly expected and mundane responses. When they got to me, I said, "I want your job."

The group was quiet for a couple of seconds. Then the vice president said, "Wow! Straight out."

I said, "Yeah, that is what I am shooting for, and I might as well not be shy about it."

After the meeting, I was approached by some lower-level executives, and they said they were really proud of what I said, as it took a lot of guts, and that it was important to speak up when you want things. They went on to say that there were senior-level people they'd like me to meet.

From that meeting, I secured a lot of contacts and made a name for myself at the company in just a few months. I got invited by several senior managers to participate in a number of different special projects. This all happened because I decided to have some guts and speak up.

Everybody needs something—that is the way the world works. We all need help, and we need resources. Don't be afraid to reach out to people when you need something, but on the other end of the spectrum, understand that you need to be open to reciprocate when those individuals need your assistance.

Being a proactive communicator involves networking like crazy. Build up a network of people in your field in the areas where you are trying to optimally perform. If you are speaking on a particular topic in economics, develop a network with the top economics people and groups. Get to know them, get to know where they socialize, and find out what they are all about so you can have the best information available.

Must-Have Communication Skills

You need to develop, mature, and cultivate the following communication skills if you are going to be able to perform at your optimum best.

Effective Written-Communication Skills

Effective written communication is a vital and important skill. You need to be able to write clearly, effectively, and concisely in a format that people can easily understand. When writing letters, memos, e-mails, agendas, and status notes, you need to ensure proper grammar and spelling and that you deliver accuracy in every line.

Effective Oral-Communication Skills

Oral communication, while primarily referring to spoken verbal communication, can also involve visual aids and nonverbal elements to support the conveyance of meaning. Oral communication includes speeches, presentations, discussions, and aspects of interpersonal communication. As a type of face-to-face communication, body language and tone play significant roles and may have greater impact on the listener than informational content. This type of communication also garners immediate feedback.

Effective Listening Skills

Another important area is listening skills. I mentioned earlier to shut up and listen, and for good reason. Listening is important so you can gather the proper requirements, guidelines, and rules. If you talk too much or want people to see you and hear you, then you might potentially miss key information.

Effective Presentation Skills

In many cases, excellent presentation skills will be critical to your success. You need to be able to put together presentations that are organized, flow right, and are the right duration, and use the right inflection in your voice. Make sure you are prepared when you present, because this is what the customer or client expects.

General Office Skills

Written communication can also involve knowing how to utilize office tools to maximize your efficiency and effectiveness. The most common communication office tools are used for word processing, producing spreadsheets and charts, and creating presentations. Having good skills in Microsoft Word, Excel, and PowerPoint will make things much easier overall.

Group Skills Dynamics

Being able to function and communicate in a group is crucial when you deal with complex subjects such as technology, finance, planning, strategy development, and other areas. When participating in such groups, you want to be an active and contributing member rather than an observer or spectator.

In my career in the corporate and business worlds, I've been involved in several group projects. While each was different, my knowledge about group dynamics and how to deal with different people enabled me to be a successful contributor to these groups.

Understanding the dynamics of the group process involves areas such as membership participation; leadership decision making; group morale; group sensitivities, strengths and weaknesses; personality conflicts; and member commitment. The term "group process" refers to how group members work together and get things done. Membership in a group enables people to develop interpersonal communication skills, establish self-assurance, and build relationships as they work to accomplish the group's overall goal.

I've had several opportunities to be a contributing member in a group. For example, when I was getting my MBA, I took a business-law class where I was paired up with a young lady named Nina. Although Nina was nice, bright, and intelligent, she turned out to be a poor group partner. Unfortunately, she had all sorts of personal problems.

For the project, we needed to research a legal subject, do a write-up, and present our findings to the class. Initially when we met to divide the tasks, we had a good session and evenly divided the work between us. However, as time went on, I couldn't get in contact with Nina. I continued to do my part but got concerned with her lack of communication. A couple of weeks went by, and Nina finally showed up to class, and said she had not been able to do anything because of her personal issues. However, she promised to get her part done in the final week.

As the next few days went by, Nina confessed that she couldn't complete the project. In fact, she did not even know or understand what was needed because she simply had no time to concentrate on school. Obviously, this infuriated me, as I would have liked to have known this three weeks prior. I reported her behavior to the professor, and he said he would have nothing to do with it, as that was part of group dynamics and working with partners. He said the expectation was still the same, no excuses.

Although I knew it would be nearly impossible for me to cover all of Nina's work in the next couple of days, I went to work. At this point, I totally shut her out. It was my project and my project alone. When it came time to present, Nina showed up and stood up in front of the class during the presentation. Everything she said was gibberish. However, it gave the class and the instructor an appearance that we worked together. Needless to say, this was not my best work because there were simply too many gaps, and the instructor managed to find all of them. I got my only C in the MBA program.

From that point, my relationship with Nina soured. When I saw her on campus, I didn't speak to her. I even said disparaging remarks about her to other students, warning them not to be on projects with her, as she would leave them hanging. So the group dynamics failed to work in this case.

Later on, I was enrolled in a microeconomics class. I was also starting a new job in Disney. I didn't have any time for school, as the job had me working all day and nights and weekends, as Disney was preparing its websites for the upcoming Christmas season. At that time, online stores made up to 80 percent of the company's yearly revenue during Christmas, so this was make-or-break time at work.

As it turned out, the instructor assigned a major project, breaking the class up into groups of four. At first, I got along well with the group. I made the group meetings and was meeting my assignments. Then things kept coming up. I missed a meeting, and then two. As time went on, I couldn't count how many meetings I was missing. I said to myself, "Oh no, I've become the new Nina," and, indeed, I turned out to be the group member who didn't contribute. Pretty soon, the team stopped inviting me to the group meetings. In their minds, I was no longer part of the group, as I wouldn't show up for the practice meetings and practice sessions. When we did our final presentation, it turned out to be one of the most embarrassing moments during my MBA. They didn't include my name and didn't have a part for me to say. However, I, like Nina, stood up in front of the class right next to the group to show the students and instructor that I was part of them. I didn't say much, but I added just enough to be convincing. It was embarrassing and shameful. However, it was a true learning experience of how not to treat people in your group and how not to be treated.

It hurts when you don't do your part, and you let your team down. It hurts when the team knows it, and they become tired of your excuses. I basically did a minimal amount of work to help me survive, but I was not a real contributing member of the team. The team did not like me anymore and didn't feel I was part of them.

Communications Pillar Final Thoughts

Communications impact every facet of performance. To perform, you need to understand who to communicate with and how. It is also imperative to understand what communication tools and techniques are readily available and effective.

The next pillar, Desire, will focus on a trait that is often overlooked. Desire is difficult to measure objectively, but it is easy to see. Understanding how desire and passion feed into optimum performance is essential for getting you to unleash the beast in you.

CHAPTER 10

You Gotta Want It

Pillar Six: Desire

While watching the 2012 Olympics, I was struck by how many medal-winning athletes attributed their success to the hard work and dedication they had endured for the past four, eight, ten years. They explained that their one shining moment of glory was only possible through the long, rigorous, lonely hard hours of work throughout the years. To work that hard for that long takes heart, dedication, and desire. Vince Lombardi once said, "The dictionary is the only place that success comes before work. Hard work is the price we must pay for success. I think you can accomplish anything if you're willing to pay the price."

Desire is simply an inclination to want things, to wish for or crave something. Of all the EPOP™ pillars, the Desire Pillar is the differentiator. You can prepare all you want. You can get all the proper training or education, and you can practice what you've learned. However, if you don't have the desire to push yourself, the desire to work hard, the desire to go the extra mile, then you will not reach your optimum performance. Period.

When you have desire, it helps you stay focused. Desire helps you make it through the pain. Desire helps you to make it through when you're tired. Desire helps you make it through when part of you says, "I can't do it." In response, desire says, "Yes, you can. You must." Desire helps you make it through when all hope seems lost, but, in your heart, you can't quit. If you don't have enough desire, you can lack energy. Without desire, you will want to take shortcuts, take the easy or lazy route. You will not work as hard. You won't do the proper research. You won't take the proper classes and get the proper training. You simply will not go the extra mile and put in the extra effort to push yourself to optimum levels. Desire is about attitude, dedication, hard work, resilience, and heart. You know you need to give it your all in whatever you do, or you will disappoint your family, friends, and relatives, but most importantly, yourself.

When I decided to go to college several years back, it was out of a desire to make something of myself. I did not want to struggle all my life in dead-end jobs. When I was a boy growing up in the inner cities of Los Angeles, I wasn't sure what I wanted to do or what I wanted to be. I had heard of being a doctor or a lawyer or something called an engineer; however, I never really gave it much thought because I never knew anyone in those professions.

I knew a lot of blue-collar workers, such as bus drivers, janitors, custodians, contractors, and construction workers. These were the types of jobs the adults in my neighborhood typically held. I looked up to and respected these adults because they were hardworking, law-abiding people, and they had homes, cars, and money to go to dinner. However, I always felt something was missing. I often went with my family to eat at restaurants outside of our neighborhood, in so-called "affluent neighborhoods." Those areas always seemed to look cleaner, safer, newer, and just plain better. They had the stores and restaurants I saw in TV commercials. Things just looked different, and I always wanted to know why.

I also had a desire to go to places I had seen on globes and world maps. However, once again, I never heard anyone talking about going to Europe, Asia, Africa, or India. The only travel people in my neighborhood talked about were vacations within the United States. They talked about trips to Texas, Arkansas, Indiana, Mississippi, and Louisiana. But I never gave it much thought because I believed I would work hard, get a good job, and live a little better than my parents did—and they did not live that bad. I had the burning desire to live life to the fullest.

So I chose one of the toughest curriculums in school: engineering. At the time, I didn't know anyone who was an engineer. In fact, I barely knew what an engineer was or what engineers did. I just knew that this type of career would take me far. But wanting something and acquiring it are two different things, and my road to a college degree was a tough one.

As I mentioned earlier, I didn't go to college directly out of high school, as I decided, instead, to help my father start his new mortgage business in the early eighties. I believed I didn't need college to move up, because I was just as smart and clever as the kids who went to college. I didn't think I needed to spend four years in college to move up in a company (I should have read Pillar Three in my book). That was, in my humble opinion, for "suckers."

The only college experience I had was taking classes at Southwest Community College part time while I worked with my father in the mortgage business. My goal at the time was to forgo the normal college route and help my dad succeed in his business venture by working as his understudy. This sounded like a doable task, since he had a fancy office and all.

Little did I know, that was the worst time to start a mortgage business, as interest rates were 21 percent plus ten points. In addition, the potential client had to be at the same job for seven years with excellent credit. And this was in the inner city where only 1 percent of the community met those requirements. Needless to say, in six months not one person walked through the door to get a "real" loan. Several people came off the streets to "borrow" a couple of bucks, but, to this day, I don't think they've paid those loans back. This lack of foot traffic in the office was the first sign that I had made a mistake. Expectedly, I soon left my dad's business, and, for the next year and a half, I worked at a bunch of dead-end jobs. I was a sales clerk in the stationery store next to my dad's office, I sold insulation door-to-door, and I worked as a smog inspector. When I finally had enough, I decided to go full force into college.

I was excited about this new decision and hurried to Cerritos College to register. I met with a guidance counselor to help determine what classes I should take to help me on my path to becoming an engineer. To my surprise, the counselor said, "Are you sure you don't want to become a welder or something like that? Engineering is a very tough major, and welding would be a lot easier." At that moment, I could not believe what he had said. I was crushed. I kept saying to myself, "Is he right? Is he correct? Maybe that's why there aren't a lot of African Americans taking engineering. Maybe he's right, because I didn't do so well on the math assessment test. Do I really want to spend the next four to five years in a major that I'm destined to fail?"

However, that's when desire kicked in. I desired to be an engineer no matter what it took. I desired to be successful, to have a good life in a successful engineering career. I looked at that counselor and thought, *Welding...you can take that welding and...*Well, you know the rest. I told the counselor that I understood that I had challenges; however, I was going to become an engineer and not a welder, so could he please let me know what classes I should take, or did I need to get another counselor?

He looked at me and mumbled, "Well, OK, but I warned you." And the rest is history.

It was desire that kept me going on the right path. The counselor could have destroyed my dreams right there. If I did not have the burning desire to be an engineer and follow my own path, I could be doing something else right now. At the time, Desire was my strongest pillar in my quest to become an engineer. I was not adequately *prepared* for the intense engineering major (Pillar One). I didn't have the normal *skill set* or profile for an engineer (Pillar Two), as I was not one of those MIT kids from the suburbs but an above-average African American kid from Inglewood who had been out of school for a couple of years. I didn't have the appropriate *knowledge*, education, and training (Pillar Three); I had not started to *practice* my craft, since I didn't even have that training (Pillar Four), and I didn't know what my *communication* skills and tool set were (Pillar Five). But I did have *desire* and a formidable work ethic (Pillar Six). I was now *focused* on getting an education (Pillar Seven), and I began to *execute* my plan (Pillar Eight). However, it was my overall desire, willingness to do hard work, and never-say-never attitude that told me to tell the counselor to take a hike and get out of my path, because I was coming through.

Desirous People Surround Themselves with Successful People

A significant way you can impact your performance and evolve into an optimum performer is to surround yourself with people who want to succeed. This is called the "power of association," where you surround yourself with positive thinkers. Usually, successful people enhance their abilities to achieve their goals through desire. Success breeds success, and productivity creates productivity. This is why great athletes like Tiger Woods hang around greats like Michael Jordan, Charles Barkley, and Roger Federer. Laker great Magic Johnson once said that one thing that helps him to succeed is to surround himself or associate himself with people who desire and believe in winning. This ensures that you always have a positive environment around you.

The opposite is also true, as failure breeds failure and negativity breeds negativity. For some reason, criminals seem to hang with one another, and they sometimes commit crimes when they are associating with each other. Likewise, lazy people seem to like to hang around with lazy people. To be an optimum performer, surround yourself with people who desire to be successful.

Desire Means Dreaming Big

When you think of desire, think about dreaming big. Of course, you can desire small things such as french fries at McDonald's or a Java Chip Frappuccino from Starbucks, but we are talking about big things that will impact your life going forward. Desire is about what you want to achieve in life and what steps you need to take to fulfill that desire.

Desire will drive how your targeted activity will impact your life. For example, if you nail down that exam or test you are taking, how will that improve your situation? Perhaps a good grade on the test could move you closer to an *A* in the class. On the other hand, if you didn't do so well, it could be an indication that more studying is needed. Therefore, an *A* in the class can lead to greater things and move you closer to fulfilling your desired dreams.

Likewise, if you have a presentation or a speech coming up, you know that if you do well in this, it could mean a business opportunity or maybe a promotion. If you nail that interview, you could get the job you have been seeking, which would further move you toward your dreams.

For a sports-related example, say your desire is to improve your golf score by ten points. This would change your golf livelihood in several ways: golf would be more enjoyable, you could play more frequently, and you could play more challenging and beautiful courses. So having desire helps fuel you in going after your dream.

Desire and Motivation

You need to be internally and/or externally motivated by something to fulfill those dreams and to get what you desire. The "something" that motivates you could be money, an award, a milestone, a pat on the back, or it could be just fulfilling other goals. However, something needs to motivate you to really give you the desire to fuel the completion of the activity.

In some cases, you may have most of what you desire; however, you have a "burning" desire to complete something that you've been trying for some time but can't seem to get over the hump. For example, LeBron James, possibly the greatest basketball player in the twenty-first century, moved to the Miami Heat from the Cleveland Cavaliers specifically to get the one thing he was not able to achieve in Cleveland, and that was an NBA championship. He had already achieved most of what he wanted to in his career: he had done everything in the game of basketball, he had won several MVPs, he has been the scoring leader for years, and he had made a ton of money. But the one thing that was missing from his illustrious career was a championship.

So LeBron James had a desire to get that championship, and he worked hard at trying to attain that goal. In order to fulfill that burning desire, he prepared extensively, he made sure he possessed the needed skill set, and he accumulated an extensive knowledge of the game. He kept practice regimens that were far and above most people's. He had a communication element in place. The area that many people questioned about him was desire. Did he have the desire to win that championship? In 2012, LeBron James and the Miami Heat did fulfill the desire by winning the NBA championship. He is, officially, "a beast."

Olympic athletes—what motivates them? There is no money for most of them at the end of the rainbow, but it is that desire to be the best, to accomplish feats that few people have accomplished. So there are all different levels of things that motivate you, and they all stem from the burning desire to achieve, be successful, and reach your optimum potential and optimum performance.

You also could be motivated in a different way, such as in an effort to prevent something negative from happening to you, such as avoiding getting fired or gaining weight. You don't want to gain weight, get sick, be poor, or get embarrassed. These are motivating factors, so you work hard so those things don't happen to you. An example of this comes from one of my favorite shows, *The Celebrity Apprentice*, where the essence of the show is to try to not get fired. (On the noncelebrity version of *The Apprentice*, there is a positive motivation as well, where if they win it all, it amounts to riches, opportunities, and unbelievable access to a great network of entrepreneurs. Reality shows in general are great examples of desire and the need to perform well and to seek goals that you know may not be realized.)

Desire can push you to go the extra mile. It enables you to practice five more minutes than you thought about practicing. It drives you to hit twenty more golf balls than you planned, because you have been pushed by the desire to do well. You edit the paper one more time because you are being pushed by desire. It pushes you to go over the speech or the sales pitch again and again. You can have a desire to get out of your current job and into a new one if it doesn't fulfill the dream you envision. You can have a desire to live in a great neighborhood and dreams of traveling the world.

I had dreams of traveling the world, and those were some of the goals that pushed my desire to do the things I needed to do. I had a desire to become an engineer, a desire to be in software development, to be an entrepreneur, and to be in management, and all of those goals were pushed by my desire to make them happen, and all those things came true.

Desire and Passion

"Passion" involves having a strong feeling for someone or something. In general, having passion is considered a positive thing, but sometimes passion can become obsession, and that can be a problem. Passion is important, because, without it, it is hard to stay motivated. You need passion to drive you to work harder to learn something. You need passion to give you the strength to tough out the hard days at work. You need to be passionate about something just for the love of it. Generally, people who love what they are doing or are interested in what they are trying to achieve are far more successful. In most cases, passionate people are far better performers than those who are just going through the motions.

You know you are passionate if you love it, if you think about it all day, if it is a driving force, if it is the thing that wakes you up in the morning, if it is that thing that you long for all day, or if it is the "let me finish whatever I am doing, so I can get to that thing." All that is passion. Passion means that you love what you are doing no matter if you get paid for it, or get paid little for it, or get paid a lot for it. Besides the passion of learning about my religion and learning about my faith, the other things I am passionate about are writing, golfing, cooking, and traveling around the world.

One way to find your passion is by taking a good hard look at your life. Ask yourself, what makes you happy. What gets you excited to get up in the morning? A different career choice? Volunteer work? Becoming a parent? Art? Driving a school bus? So many choices are available in life. The things that make your heart pound are your passions. Take advantage of things to be passionate about.

For me, playing golf is a passion. I could play golf every day if I had the time and money. If I'm mentally and physically able, God willing, I will play golf until I pass away. Cooking is also a passion. I would love to open up a restaurant and cook some of my favorite dishes someday.

Travel is another passion of mine and is always on my mind. Traveling to new countries, experiencing different cultures, and meeting different people in diverse areas are stimulating to me intellectually, spiritually, and physically. Understanding the way that different countries relate to one another is a passion of mine.

So "passion" is almost similar to hobbies, but it is so much more. It is what really drives you to perform because you just simply love to do it, and you are simply interested in it, and it is something that normally is within you.

Desire and Attitude

Attitude cannot be underestimated. Attitude is everything. It is the game changer. In many situations, attitude is more important than skill. Attitude is a point of view about a certain situation. Attitude is made up of basically three different components:

1. what you think
2. what you do
3. what you feel

You also have an emotional response to attitude, and you behave in a certain way because of it. Attitude is an area that can change everything. You can do all the other pillars—the planning, communication, all of that—and still get to a point where your attitude is bad: you don't like life; you don't like this; you do not like this person; you don't want to be there. These are bad attitudes, and they can ruin all of the good things you have done. If your attitude is bad, you need to begin changing it, either by changing your thinking, the way you act, or the way you feel. Don't underestimate the importance of attitude.

For example, at work a coworker may be the best in the field and may be perceived as being the top producer and employee in the company. However, if that person has a bad attitude and is someone no one can get along with, the good performance will be negated by the bad attitude.

One year when I was coaching youth football, I had a good coaching staff— great guys, with positive attitudes. They were happy to come to practice to work with the kids, and they were happy to be coaching their sons and spending time with them. But we had one coach who was knowledgeable about the game of football, yet he did not get along with the rest of the coaches. He simply appeared to have a bad attitude. He put down the other coaches and embarrassed them, and it got to the point the other coaches did not want to be around him.

Therefore, I had a dilemma. On one hand, I had a coach with all the skills to teach the kids, but he had a bad attitude. On the other hand, I had coaches who did not have the same skills (which they could pick up quickly and easily), but they had great attitudes. Then one day, one of the coaches came to me and said that he could no longer work with that coach, and that either the other coach went, or he would. I had to get rid of the bad-attitude coach.

Having a positive attitude is important in your life. A positive attitude helps you cope with the daily grind of life.

With a positive mind-set, you try to not let things bother you. In other words, you choose your attitude, and you have the power to change it at any given moment. Life becomes easier once you combine positive thinking and attitude. To exercise positive thinking, tell yourself that you are in control of your destiny and that you are going to be happy, and nothing will change that. If you have that kind of attitude about life, then great things start happening to your life. A positive attitude makes things happier, nicer, and brighter, and, in the end, you will come out on top in most everything you are involved in as you strive to reach optimum performance.

For example, while going to community college, I lived in a garage for three years in an inner-city part of Los Angeles County called Compton. In my neighborhood, Compton lived up to its challenging reputation of being a tough city where poverty and high crime rates were visible and evident. To get money, I worked the night shift in downtown Los Angeles, so I had to catch the bus at eleven at night on the Compton streets to go to work. It was scary, as all types of people walked the streets like zombies. Most of the people were on drugs or looking for them, and I never knew if someone would try to jack me. So I sometimes carried a little knife with me. Anything could've happened, but I was doing all of this to make it through my early years of college, as I was on a budget.

What got me through this was the burning desire to succeed. I had to go through tough times to really appreciate things, suck it up, and realize my overall goals and aspirations. I had to have a positive attitude about that situation, knowing things would get better. Desire and a good attitude drove me forward. This attitude allowed me to continue to believe that I would be successful and that things would turn around. I just needed to keep going and continue to go to school, focus on my goal to become an engineer, and make it through this rough patch in my life, and things would get better if I believed. And, as things turned out, it did get better.

Another example comes from a time when I joined a large global consulting firm after working at TRW for around five years as an experienced engineer. At that time, the consulting firm hired a great number of recent college graduates. These new hires had graduated at the top of their classes, usually from the most prestigious and well-known colleges in the country. In addition, they were basically the entitled, type-A people who usually got what they wanted in life. They were the types who had no problem bossing anyone around to get what they wanted.

Therefore, the challenge for me was to work with these people, and in many cases, I took direction and orders from people who were younger, more immature, and less experienced than me. It felt as if I had taken several steps back in my career. However, my positive attitude kept me going. It was the belief that I came to the company to learn, to be challenged, and to work with the best and brightest people in the industry. It was my opportunity to work for one of the top companies in the world. I remembered my goals and aspirations for the job, and those thoughts kept me in a positive frame of mind. In the end, because of my positive attitude, I grew to love my tenure at the consulting company, and, before I left, I picked up some valuable skills that I could take to my next opportunity.

Desire and Heart

Vince Lombardi once said, "Once a man has made a commitment to a way of life, he puts the greatest strength in the world behind it. It is something we call Heart Power. Once a man has made this commitment, nothing will stop him short of success." Heart is about determination and stopping at nothing to reach your goal. Heart gives you the ability to come back from adverse circumstances. If something bad happens to you, and you don't know how you'll respond and are thinking about quitting, heart offers you the ability to come back and stride forward with passion and desire to keep going. Even in the face of defeat or when you didn't achieve your goal or didn't get the result you want, heart gives you the determination to go back and try it again until you succeed. Heart is not about skill or preparation; it's about determination and perseverance to keep you going.

A classic example of heart and determination is the story of a quarterback with the New England Patriots in the NFL named Tom Brady. One could argue that Tom Brady is one of the greatest quarterbacks to ever play the game. However, he initially wasn't forecast to have a successful career in the NFL. When Brady left the Michigan Wolverines to go to the NFL, he was drafted in the sixth round of the

2000 draft. Usually, the great quarterbacks are drafted in the first couple of rounds, not in the sixth round. In fact, six quarterbacks were chosen before him. Now that Brady is a great player, those six quarterbacks are often referred to as the "'Brady Six." None of them are still playing in the NFL, and only one, Marc Bulger, had any success.

Brady had that competitor spirit and positive attitude that set him apart from the other highly sought-after athletes who were drafted ahead of him. According to a *NY Daily News* article called "Story of Boy Named Tom Brady" by Rich Cimini, Brady didn't start playing football until the ninth grade, and he was not good enough to start as quarterback on a team that was ranked eighth. That team didn't even score touchdowns, and he wasn't good enough to be the starting quarterback. The article explains that most of the people in Brady's life thought that his best sport was actually baseball, but he practically willed himself into a football career. He was a middle-class kid who was driven and focused and quietly confident (Cimini 2008).

Many football players who have played the game have said that Tom Brady is what an American athlete should be, yet he barely made the NFL. For much of his high-school and college careers, he was a backup quarterback. In addition to being selected in the sixth round, and besides the six quarterbacks taken in the draft before, there were 198 players who were chosen before him. Really?

A scouting report showed that Tom Brady was lucky to even be drafted. The draft report stated that he lacked mobility, he was very thin, he did not have a great muscular build, he could not get away from a football rush, and he could not throw that far because his arm was not considered to be strong. Those were all the scouting reports for him, and those are the reasons he was drafted so low. Tom Brady was devastated by being drafted so low and that there had been the possibility of not being drafted at all, and so he made it his life's goal to excel and exceed beyond the expectations of those who doubted his potential.

And did he ever prove the doubters wrong and rise above all expectations. As of 2014, he played in six Super Bowls, winning four of them. He was the MVP in three of those Super Bowls, and he was selected to ten Pro Bowls. He holds the NFL record for most touchdown passes in a single season, and he has a career playoff record of twenty-one and eight. He has also held the longest consecutive win streak in the NFL: twenty-one wins over two seasons. He and Joe Montana are the only two players in NFL history to have won multiple NFL, MVP, and Super-Bowl MVP awards.

So when you look at his story, it is the tale of hard work and success. Despite all the odds against him, he found a way to prove himself to the world and make the best of the situation. That is where heart comes in—Brady showed true heart. He also showed work effort, dedication, commitment, desire, and passion. After being down, being devastated, he picked himself up and rose to the occasion to become one of the greatest football players ever. This is a true story of heart.

Desire and Stick-to-itiveness

Anyone who has played golf for any length of time surely understands "stick-to-itiveness." Stick-to-itiveness is about staying with something that continues to present a challenge; despite the difficulty, you continue to stick to it until you get it right. This is also known as perseverance, which is to try and try again and not give up. Stick-to-itiveness is one of those characteristics that may not be on the radar of winning people in any profession, but perhaps it should be. You cannot really define it, because it is that "thing," that rare type of quality that, despite your experience, is a good gauge of an optimum performer. Stick-to-itiveness is about having determination against sometimes long odds and continuously getting back up after being knocked down again and again.

As I mentioned earlier, Tom Brady stuck with playing football, although his career didn't appear to be promising. Many actors have to go to hundreds of auditions, callbacks, false alerts, and unreturned calls before they get a break. Sometimes actors do only commercials for five to ten years without the promise of getting on a television show or movie, but they continue to stick it out and persevere. Former NFL quarterback Kurt Warner worked in a store bagging groceries and performed other odd jobs while playing in the lower-level, semipro football leagues before he got his shot in the NFL. Through stick-to-itiveness, he became an NFL star.

In 2004 in Athens, Greece, track star Allyson Felix had trained all her life to win a gold medal in the Olympics. She came close, as she received a silver—good, but not great. Since she wouldn't stop until she got the gold, she decided to train four more years and compete in the 2008 Olympics in Beijing, China. Again, she was only able to get a silver medal. This time she was older and more disappointed, as another four years would be a difficult road. However, in the 2012 Olympics in London, she finally won an individual gold medal in the two hundred meters as her stick-to-itiveness finally paid off. Stick-to-itiveness is about commitment, hard work, patience, endurance, and goal setting.

Long before we got married, my wife dreamed of becoming a doctor. Early in our marriage, she studied hard to be an MD; however, it was not to be, as she had challenges with some of the science courses. Later, she took classes to become a physician's assistant. As it turned out, she didn't have the same passion and desire as she had for being a doctor, so she did not continue on. Through the years, she volunteered at hospitals and even went to get her Emergency Medical Technician (EMT) certification. Finally, after a couple of decades of dreaming and perseverance, my wife fulfilled the beast in her by receiving a doctorate in psychology.

My final year of college was a trying and tough year for me. My mom had already been diagnosed with cancer, and during school, that weighed heavily on my mind. You need to first understand that that I was very close to my mom. I was what you would consider a "mama's boy"—I loved and adored her. She was my cheerleader; she was my everything. As the year went by, her health got worse, and my classes got more difficult. I needed to make a decision, as trying to concentrate on both challenges caused me to not do either well. I was not spending the appropriate amount of time with my mom, and I was not spending enough time with my studies either.

I thought about quitting school for a year to be with my mom, so I talked to her about it. I asked her what she wanted me to do: quit school and stay with her, or go full steam ahead with school until it was finished. She said, "No, I want you to finish school." She said, "Whatever you do, finish school, and graduate as an engineer. It is not only your dream; it is my dream to have my son graduate as an engineer." She went on to say, "You are going to be an engineer, a black engineer no less, and I do not want to be a barrier to your degree. Go out there, and do what you need to do. Don't worry about me. I love you, and I couldn't be more proud that you are my baby, my son. Go get it!"

I took that to heart, and I didn't quit school. I kept going. I checked in periodically, and, as her health continued to deteriorate, I continued with my studies and got closer to graduating.

My graduation was scheduled for May 25, 1990, and, on May 15 of that year, my lovely mother sadly passed away. Her passing happened right in the middle of finals, and although every bone in my body told me to stop and go home and prepare the funeral services and be with the family, I knew I had to continue studying and preparing for finals. I had to push my emotions down to the pit of my soul and suck it up. This was my final chance. If I missed finals, I would probably have to take all the classes again and wait another semester before graduating. It was a critical point in my life, and with a grieving heart. I stuck to it and did not quit. I went on through and took the exams, and got my bachelor of science in engineering despite burying my mom just before my graduation.

This is a prime example of how things can get in your way that could cause you to quit on your goals. But if you have your internal motivation, if you have dreams, goals, desire, passion, and belief in yourself, then you can unleash the beast in you and be what you want to be. Don't ever let anyone hold your beast down.

Desire and Hard Work

Many times, the difference between winning and losing, staying in average mode or moving to beast mode, comes down to who wants it the most, and who is willing to work the hardest to get the prize. Hard work can be the differentiator, because oftentimes competitors may have comparable skills, education, and training, so the only thing that separates them is the willingness to get down and dirty and do the work necessary to be a beast in that particular field.

When you think of great basketball teams in the NBA, several franchises come to mind. The Boston Celtics, Chicago Bulls, and Los Angeles Lakers have ALL demonstrated great talent and desire throughout their individual championships. However, all three franchises are also known for their team play and extreme work ethics. In fact, during the Doc Rivers coaching era, he consistently taught and instilled a hard work, maximum effort, and "leave it on the floor" mentality. Whatever activity you choose, do it with maximum effort and do it in beast mode. Do not go at it a halfway level or three-quarter level, but go all the way. Give it your all. Leave no stone unturned, sweat it all out, and, in the end, that hard work will pay off.

When I was just getting my bachelor's degree, I not only had to contend with a tough undergraduate degree in computer engineering, but I also worked thirty hours a week doing the graveyard shift. I didn't have any weekends, didn't watch TV (except for ESPN), didn't go to parties, and missed most family functions. Basically, I had no life during those college years. I went to school, went to work, and studied, and that's it.

One time while working for Disney, I was on a critical project that had to get done before one of their movies came out. In reality, the project would take six weeks to complete with a heavily loaded development staff. The problem was that the show opened in two weeks. This was a project that had to get done before the opening and not a minute after.

This was no time to complain about schedules, workloads, or a lack of resources; we simply had to perform and complete the task at hand. So I worked day and night, literally, on this project. There were no start times and end times—it was just full-speed-ahead work. It was hard and complex, and there were many times when I wanted to say F&*^%% this and suffer the consequences, but we all kept going. There were many nights that I didn't even go home. In fact, there were some times where I worked three, four straight days without going home, just working around the clock, drinking coffee, eating takeout, staying in the office, and not getting out. I slept in the office all night, and then I cleaned up in the restroom before anyone came in. The cleaning people knew me by name, but my poor wife forgot my name. This was a situation where your background, profile, education, preparation, talent, and experience don't matter. All that mattered was whether you were willing to work as hard as you could for as long as you could to meet the deadline.

In the end, we were all exhausted, but we succeeded in meeting the deadline. Disney had a fantastic opening night using this new technology, and it turned out to be a successful outcome. However, that success only came from teamwork, communication, sweat, tears, frustration, and absolute hard work.

Again consider Donald Trump's show *The Apprentice*. In the show, the goal each week is to do enough to make it to the next week and not get fired by "the Donald." During many of the weekly challenges, it is not the most well-liked, most talented, most articulate, or most educated contestants who make it through to the next week. It is usually those who work the hardest and longest, and do the most work who move to the next round and avoid getting fired. Simply put, you could be the most talented and everything else, have a great attitude and all that, but there is no replacement for working hard.

Desire and Hunger

Another aspect of desire is being hungry—not in the sense of food, but in the sense of wanting something so badly that you can virtually imagine it in your grasp, and you know that once you get a bit of that, it will satisfy you. Think of hungry lions as they quest for food. They don't stop at anything until they get that satisfying taste of whatever they have been hunting. Nothing will stop them from getting what they want. It's the same thing in your quest for your activity when things are too difficult—you can have that hunger inside you to keep going and thrive, and that will propel you to continuing in what you are trying to do.

I think of the wonderful great people of China and India. Those countries are the most populated in the world. Unfortunately, a large segment of the population has been impoverished for decades, and even centuries, due to overcrowding and fragile infrastructure. However, in the past two decades—primarily due to the rise in technology, science, engineering, and the Internet—both countries have become economic and technological leaders. This rise has been sparked by the sheer hunger of China and India to move from being considered developing countries to being world powers. In fact, the countries' successes have sparked even more hunger within the people to strive to become even greater by producing more engineering graduates than all other countries combined in the next decades to come.

This is a real hunger that can be spread, not only in someone's pursuit of an individual activity but to a country itself. There is a hunger in China and India to be accepted by the world community—not only just to be accepted, but to become superpowers. Selectively, Chinese and Indian citizens work longer and harder with high productivity and, currently, at a fraction of the labor cost of most Western countries, and this is driven by the extreme hunger of the people to succeed and prosper in this new world economy.

Hunger is also demonstrated by playoff sport teams trying to advance. Consider the team that for years and years goes to one level of the playoffs, and then gets knocked out. In the offseason, they might do things to prove themselves like acquire or trade different players and make other necessary moves to get better and better and better, because they can taste it. They can taste that championship; they can taste it right off the grass. So they come back the next year, and then sometimes they still don't make it, but sometimes they are the team who finally became champions. Think of the Miami Heat in 2012. They were hungry after a disappointing end to the 2011 season. In 2012, they used that hunger to become NBA champions.

Usually, you find it takes them a couple of years to get there, and it was that hunger that kept saying, "I can taste it; I can taste it. I can do better; I can succeed. Let me follow the goal; let me continue." And then that hunger drives them to be successful and to ultimately reach that goal.

Desire and Dedication

Another component of desire involves commitment, dedication, and sacrifice. You must believe in the path that you follow, and be dedicated. "Dedication" means to continue to put your all into it, stick with it, and make it happen, with no excuses—this is what it's all about.

When I was an engineering senator in college, I was voted the most dedicated. I received that honor basically because I took the job seriously, and I wanted to be the best senator I could be. I was dedicated to being in the senate chambers and office on time, at every meeting, answering any question from the constituents (students), and being a partner and a peer to my fellow school senators. I believed that this demonstrated my dedication to the job and to the task, and doing what's needed to be a beast performer.

When trying to do your best, you must sacrifice or omit some things from your life. I mentioned earlier that when I was getting my bachelor's degree, I had to get rid of the partying, socializing, leisure time, sleep, family gatherings, and even reading a good book now and then. I had to reduce my circle of friends, and even my relationships were impacted because I had to dedicate my time to doing the things that I needed to do to accomplish my goals.

When I was in my final year, I was just as dedicated and committed to making this happen and getting this done. I couldn't drive home at night because it took too much time away, so I started sleeping in the janitor's office at the university. I showered in the school shower in the morning, and I ate breakfast in the school cafeteria. I carried different sets of clothes with me: a couple pairs of jeans (because you can wear jeans every day without anyone noticing) and a few wrinkle-free T-shirts or golf shirts. I was dedicated to making it happen and graduating. Sometimes being dedicated involves eliminating the overhead and concentrating on what's important to get the job completed.

Surround Yourself with Winners, Not Whiners

Last, but certainly not least in the area of desire, surround yourself with winners and not whiners. Surround yourself with people who will support you and be behind you. Surround yourself with people who have their own goals and successes in front of them, and not those who always complain about the government; missed opportunities; or their bosses, spouses, kids, and life in general. You should try to get away from those negative influences and surround yourself with positive thinkers. When you do that, you are more apt to produce positive results.

Surrounding yourself with negative influences can have the opposite impact on your success and performance. Negative people definitely have a negative impact on those within their vicinity. In contrast, winning teams consist of people who, as a group, believe in succeeding. So if you are trying to go in the right direction to achieve your goal and attain an optimum performance, then you need to get rid of negative people and pessimistic influences in your life, and surround yourself with positive people who believe in you and inspire you.

As Oprah Winfrey said, "Surround yourself with only people who are going to lift you higher." If you surround yourself with excellent and honorable people, they can only elevate you. If you surround yourselves with people who are *not* excellent and honorable, they will pull you down into the world of mediocrity, and they will keep you there as long as you allow them to.

Desire Pillar Final Thoughts

Desire and passion are major fuel components that drive top performers to accomplish more than expected. Without desire, you won't reach optimum performance.

Optimum performance requires all your attention and awareness. If your brain is concentrating on something other than your target goals, then something will eventually fall through the cracks and overall performance will suffer. This next chapter, Focus Pillar, will help you keep your eyes and mind on the prize.

CHAPTER 11

'N Da Zone

Pillar Seven: Focus

Da Hill

'm what some would call a "recreational" runner or jogger. I run about three to four times a week and go to the gym the other days. My home is located in an area with plenty of hills, and most of my running routes have some type of hill component.

One day, I decided to do a longer-than-normal run of seven or eight miles (usually, I do three to five miles). The route I selected had a major hill at the end. In previous attempts at this hill, it was difficult for me to make it up to the top without stopping for a break (or two). It was a scary, long, and steep hill that was challenging on normal runs. For some reason, though, I felt I was ready for this hill, even after a longer run where my legs would be totally spent.

As I began my journey, I made good progress (better than expected). After six and a half grueling miles in the sun, I had one mile to go with this monstrous hill still to climb. As I approached the hill, I looked up and thought that the only way I would make it up without stopping would be to focus on the goal of reaching the top. I needed to first get the negative thoughts out of my head and think only of a successful outcome.

As I started up the hill, my legs tightened under the extreme gravitational pull of the hot pavement. My heart beat faster as it attempted to pump more oxygen into my tired, aching, and sore muscles. To keep my composure, I zoned in and blocked everything out. I focused on each step; I looked down at the squares on the pavement and focused on putting each foot in the next square, one by one. Step by step, I challenged the hill by focusing on the square in front of me and not looking up to the top. If I would have looked up, I could have gotten discouraged by how long the journey up the hill remained, and that would have been a huge distraction.

Unfortunately, my path crossed about three hundred yards of angry and hungry honeybees. Amazingly, I did not get distracted by the bees as they kept hitting my legs and arms, buzzing around my face and ears, and sticking to my clothes. I paid them no attention because I continued to focus on the goal. I continued on as if they were not there. I was in a zone.

As I continued up the hill, other distractions vied for my attention. Cars beeped their horns at me, dogs barked as if I were their next meal, and other runners and bikers littered my path. But I continued to focus and didn't let these distractions hinder my progress and throw me off course. I didn't even look to my right or left in fear that landmarks would give me a clue as to how far I was from the end. I just looked down and straight ahead. I only focused on the goal of getting up the hill.

Although the pain in my legs increased, the air in my lungs became more difficult to retain, and the sweat dripped down my face, I continued to focus and block everything out. Eventually, I succeeded and conquered that hill, even with all the obstacles and distractions. I was able to maintain my focus, and that's why I succeeded.

With so many distractions around us, staying focused can be a real challenge. Yet it will take focus for you to achieve optimum performance in anything. Being productive means being focused. One of the main reasons people struggle to perform in their business, academic, athletic, professional, and personal endeavors is simply a lack of focus. This lack of focus can be pricy. It makes achieving optimum performance difficult, and it can stop you from getting what you want and block your true success. Imagine being focused, knowing clearly where you're heading, and consistently taking the necessary actions to get there. Being focused means not wandering off topic and sticking to what's important.

Losing focus on your goals and objectives is the silent killer of dreams. You can have everything lined up perfectly in your preparation and training, but without focus, every time you get ready to take positive steps in your journey, something gets in the way and takes your attention away from your plan.

Distractions to Look For

Sometimes the distractions are big ones, such as when you suddenly have a heavier-than-expected workload, illness in the family or with yourself, loss of a job, move to a new location, and other such life-changing events—things that have the potential to seriously disrupt whatever plans you have. For example, during my college years, my mom's illness was a major distraction that I had to deal with in order to meet my goals.

In addition to major distractions, there are also medium-level distractions that sometimes get in the way. This type of distraction might include partying instead of studying, or socialize at the gym rather than actually exercising. Another example is when you are about to study, train, or practice, and then friends or family show up unexpectedly at your doorstep. Many of these distractions are uncontrollable; however, they distract or temporarily take you away from your progress, causing you to lose focus.

There are also small distractions that cause you to lose focus. Interestingly, the small ones can be more dangerous to your progress than the bigger ones, because they tend to happen more frequently and can impact your life in a silent and destructive manner. This includes such distractions as impromptu phone calls, e-mails, texts, and instant messaging where you immediately respond back. Social media such as Facebook, Twitter, and MySpace, along with Internet surfing, are also distraction vehicles that, in some cases, can be addictive and literally take you away for hours from whatever you were doing. Of course, watching television is definitely a major distraction and time stealer, as today you have cable and satellite TV where you can get hundreds of channels all day, every day.

Getting into Focus

Being focused isn't just about limiting distractions; it's about getting yourself into a zone and narrowing in on what you need to do to accomplish the task at hand. Being focused means being able to ignore those distractions that tempt you away from your path. You can allow yourself to feel these insecurities and doubts, and learn from them—to recognize them for what they are (mere distractions) and turn your heart once more to the path of your life's journey.

Being focused is potent and invites success. For many people, their focus only lasts a short while before sliding away. When you're clear about what you want to focus on, the next step is to keep that focus. Do whatever it takes to maintain it.

Learning what you need to focus on may or may not have been easy, depending on you as an individual. But the real challenge is to continue that focus day after day after day. This level of obligation is required so that momentum builds, improvement is made, and you see the positive outcomes. If you don't maintain the necessary focus, your effort will be minimal and your use of resources, including your time, will be ineffective.

In order to focus, you must be able to prioritize, limit distractions, and get into a zone, and then you need to put everything together. There are two types of focus in the overall activity: the before-execution focus and the during-execution focus.

Before-Execution Focus

The "before-execution focus" involves everything that you do leading up to the actual event, performance, activity, or act. This is the state in which you prepare, plan, organize, research, and gather analysis on your competition. You need to prioritize, and you need to focus everything to be able to adequately prepare for game time. You need to continue to sharpen your focus up until it's time to execute by doing your presentation or speech, performing in a game, submitting a paper, or taking a test.

Prioritize

As you prepare to execute an activity or task, it is important to ensure you have prioritized the activities in your daily life. These "daily life" activities are usually the schedule drivers that will impact your ability to perform on your target activity. Some examples of these daily activities may include the following:

Family Life

- chauffeuring kids to and from school, rehearsals, and sporting events
- preparing daily meals
- household chores (e.g., cleaning the house)
- parent meetings
- kids' homework
- paying bills
- running errands
- exercising and working out

Work

- job activities
- meetings

- phone calls
- administrative functions
- training

Church Functions

- attending church services
- Bible study
- choir rehearsals
- ministry meetings

All these types of activities happen in your normal everyday life, and you need to manage them correctly before focusing your energy on the target activity. Once you're able to manage the "life" priorities, start focusing on the target activity through:

- preparation
- research
- planning
- practicing
- communicating
  - sending e-mails
  - getting everybody engaged

Whatever you need to do, this is the time to focus.

Also, when prioritizing, limit the amount on your plate. Since there are only twenty-four hours in a day, you need to prioritize. You can't take on activities that will take twenty-six hours to do—something must be removed.

Your first step is to identify all the activities on your plate. At this point, use the skills learned in Pillar One regarding organization and time management. The goal is to organize your life to accommodate the activities in your life and prioritize them so you can get maximum benefit and performance.

Limit Distractions

The next part you need to manage in the before-execution focus state is your distractions. By limiting distractions, you move everything out of the way in your head and in your life so that you can focus on getting your performance ready. When you start your preparation activities and begin working on your planning and organization, you need to limit the distractions and clear a path for you to have a centered mind to accomplish your goals. For instance, to limit distractions while you are doing preparation work, get everything ready before you sit down:

- Take a nap before you sit down and start prep work, not during prep. Watch out for weariness. If you start getting tired, this also limits your focus.
- Get all your snacks together beforehand.
- Eat beforehand. Being hungry is one of the major obstacles to staying focused.
- Get your coffee ready before you settle in.
- If you have to go to the bathroom, take care of that.
- Take care of all your phone conversations.
- Clean up your work area.
- Make your environment comfortable. Make sure that the temperature where you are studying is just right, adjusting the air conditioner, fan, or heater to your preferred level.
- Put on some headphones, and listen to music without lyrics, such as jazz or classical. Do not put on music with lyrics, because you might find yourself singing along with it and can start losing focus that way. However, background music puts you into a mood and sharpens your mind. Turn off the TV.
- Limit Internet usage, including searching and browsing, and online shopping. When you check your e-mail, try not to stray and read things on the Internet because pretty soon you'll have clicked away and wasted thirty minutes or so. So be careful when you check e-mail. It's preferable that you don't check at all while you are focusing, but if you have to, keep it limited.
- Limit social networking. Avoid sites like Twitter and Facebook while you are in focus because they take you out of focus, and it is hard to get back.
- Avoid instant messaging and texting. These types of communication will take you away from whatever you plan on doing to prepare yourself for the activity.

Get into the Zone

Once you get all those nasty distractions out of the way, it's time to get into the zone. Think about your life. The daily segments of your life are not much different from those of others. Everyone has twenty-four hours each day, whether you are a convict in prison or the CEO of a major corporation. What you do with that time is what's important. Everyone must set aside time to sleep, anywhere from four to ten hours daily. Aside from sleep, most people's lives consist of daily life segments such as work or school, transportation, entertainment, family affairs, eating, community involvement, self-improvement, and doing nothing. When you get into a zone, you need to ensure you get the most out of each daily life segments and that they are properly allocated (i.e., eight hours of work, eight hours of sleep, and so on).

You need to have the correct daily life segment balance in your life. For example, maybe you shouldn't be working, but should be in school to improve your chances of getting a better job. Or perhaps your entertainment daily life segment is too large at eight hours—in other words, you're having too much *fun*—and your sleep is only three hours. This imbalance will probably cause performance problems in other areas, such as work.

To get into the zone, you need to start conditioning your mind:

- Restate the mission.
- Restate the goals.
- Restate the objective.
- Concentrate on the goal.
- Set up your boundaries and limitations, and try to stay between those lines.

Put It All Together
Finally, put all the above focus items together. You want to prioritize everything you are doing in your life, limit the distractions, and get yourself to a zone so you are ready to work.

During-Execution Focus (Day Of)

"During execution" refers to the actual day that you do your activity: give the presentation or speech, play the game, or host the event. At the time of execution, pay attention to each one of these things:

1. prioritize
2. limit distractions
3. get yourself in to a zone
4. put it all together

Prioritize

This is the actual day, so you need to prioritize your life to make sure that you have enough time to focus on what you need to do. Let's use the example of a presentation. To prioritize, you need to:

- Clear your calendar and your BlackBerry or iPhone.
- Make sure you have enough time set aside.
- Make sure there is nothing scheduled right before the presentation that will distract you or weigh on your mind.
- Limit or cancel any meetings or appointments one hour before and one hour after you execute the activity.

Limit Distractions

The next thing is to limit the distractions, similar to what you did during the pre-execution phase. This is important, as limiting distractions will create a positive wall around you. Be sure to only tell your inner circle you are doing the presentation, as this will help lessen the pressure and the expectations.

Get into the Zone

To get yourself into the zone on the day of execution, you need to:

- get ready
- relax
- control your breathing
- review
- rehearse, and get yourself ready
- get yourself into the moment

Focus Pillar Final Thoughts

Put It All Together. Now is the time to put it all together—game on. This is when you take action, and you go in, you do it, and you apply yourself. Once you have your mind focused on this particular activity, you are ready to execute.

CHAPTER 12

Lights, Camera, Show Time—Make It Happen!

Pillar Eight: Execution

Vince Lombardi used to say, "Fundamentals win it. Football is two things: It's blocking and tackling. If you block and tackle better than the other team, you're going to win. Execute the fundamentals, and the rest will follow." In order to unleash the beast in you and achieve optimum performance in whatever activity you choose, you need to execute the fundamental aspects of these eight pillars. The fundamental aspects of EPOP™ are: preparation, skill set, knowledge, practicing, communicating, desire and passion, and focus. Once you have all those aspects developed, you must actually *do* something. That's what execution is about—the actual *doing* of the activity. What determines if you will actually reach optimum performance depends on how well you execute.

This is the only pillar that really matters. The other pillars are designed to help you execute. If you did none of them and still won the championship, got an optimum score on an exam, had a winning presentation or sales pitch, or submitted a beast of a proposal, then you didn't need the other pillars (although this is highly unlikely). On the other hand, if you did all the other pillars very well, but the execution was subpar, then the effort failed, and you would need to reevaluate your strategy. Execution is all that counts in the end.

In basketball, a coach might design the perfect play that gets the ball into the best player's hand to take the winning shot. However, if the players do not run the play correctly and turn over the ball or are forced to get it to a secondary player, then they did not flawlessly execute the well-designed play, and Pillar Eight failed.

This gap between using fundamentals and the execution of those fundamentals is called the "execution gap." A primary goal of EPOP™ is to close or mitigate the execution gap as much as possible. Closing the execution gap is one of the most challenging actions of anyone trying to achieve optimum performance. A person can set out to implement a plan or project and only realize a portion of the desired effect. When you have a large execution gap, you may be able to perform "best effort," but it is difficult to achieve optimum performance. The Execution Pillar is designed to help EPOP™ seekers close the execution gap. The key difference between "best effort" performance and "optimum" performance often lies in the ability to execute. This is the pillar to get it done. It's about winning, closing the deal. You can only reach beast mode if you close the deal.

For example, you see this all the time—coaches who have done well throughout the season and have led their team to winning records. These are coaches who win all the time during the regular season, sometimes even earning "Coach of the Year" recognition. However, when the playoffs start, those same coaches can't seem to take that team all the way to the championship, or even far into the playoffs. Although making it to the playoffs or Bowl games is a great accomplishment, team owners consider that to be a "good" performance, not an "optimum" performance for their particular teams.

Sometimes this result of achieving a good versus an optimum performance can get coaches fired. In fact, in February 2007, the San Diego Chargers fired head coach Marty Schottenheimer after getting a best record of fourteen and two. This is because the Chargers were unexpectedly knocked out of the playoffs by the New England Patriots. Of course, this seems highly unfair and rough, but to some people, the ultimate prize is to win it all, and nothing else will do. Coincidentally, as of 2015, the Chargers still haven't won the Super Bowl.

In order to get the ultimate prize, you need to execute. When the competition is stiff and the stakes are high, what usually determines who wins or loses is who best executes the plan—*not* who has the best plan. If the activity you are trying to optimally perform is of a competitive nature—such as a sport, job interview, debate, college-entrance exam—then chances are that the top competitors have implemented some or all of the other seven pillars. Thus, the final result will depend on who executes the best, who has the capacity to pull everything together at the right moment to achieve the desired results. The person who achieves that will be the optimum performer.

In the 2011 Super Bowl featuring the Pittsburgh Steelers and the Green Bay Packers, both teams essentially followed the first seven pillars to perfection.

However, in the end, it was the Green Bay Packers that executed their game plan more effectively than the Steelers, thereby getting the win.

To "execute" means to put into effect, to carry out, or to perform. In short, it means to get things done or to finish. Execution comes after you have:

- extensively prepared, planned, strategized, organized, and managed your time
- further developed your skills and knowledge through extensive training and instruction
- communicated everything you possibly can
- practiced over and over again, honing those skills, reiterating those skills, and repeating the skills
- displayed the desire, passion, and eagerness to get things done, a willingness to sweat the pain
- arrived in a place you can focus and limit your distractions

When all this is done, **it's game time, and it's time to unleash the beast in you.**

The Three Phases of Execution

Execution is about getting things done. It's about action, about making it happen. This is the time when all the preparation, planning, organization, research, communication, and practice now come to fruition. This is when you actually have to do it, display it, or show it, and this is the part where you actually see results from all the work you've done. It's time to "unleash the beast in you."

When you have executed better than you ever have before, that means that your pillar preparation has worked and has made you a better performer than you were before. Execution is where the final results are. It tells basically everything about how far you've come. If your activity was to run in 5K and you used the pillar formula to achieve or do better in that 5K, then you'll know it worked if your time is better now than it was before you utilized the formula. That is what execution is about. It's about actually participating and making that happen.

There are three phases in execution. These are as follows:

1. Execution preparation
2. Game time (in the moment)
3. The aftermath (examining the results)

Execution Preparation

Execution preparation is about getting everything ready and prepared on the day of game time. Depending on the activity, getting ready could mean completing several different tasks leading up to your performance. The different tasks that can be done during the execution-preparation phase mainly involve three key elements:

a.   Ensuring logistics are in order
b.   Getting your body right
c.   Getting your mind right

Ensuring Logistics Are in Order

Getting yourself ready the day of the actual activity can sometimes be just as important as performing the activity itself. For example, if the activity is a presentation, then you need to ensure you have the presentation file in hand and loaded on the equipment or computer that will run it. You need to ensure that the projector is available and working properly, which should include a test run to see if the file works on the equipment in the same manner as it worked on your computer. You need to ensure you have transportation to the event, and you need to take care of the attire for the activity. Any promotional material that needs to be distributed should be set up in the designated areas.

You also need to ensure that your logistics are in order with the presentation or speech itself. Make sure you have all the paperwork and equipment lined up, your speech ready, the laptop and power cord on hand, a printout of documentation or the presentation speech, and/or your write-up cards—everything that you need. It's also recommended that you make sure you have soft copies of the documentation and the presentation, the speech, and write-up on a separate flash drive just in case something happens.

When you get to the presentation room, you need to see that the presentation works with the LED screen and projector, and that the microphone is working properly. Envision how the audience will see your presentation. Work on your voice, and see if you are projecting the way you want to. Look at your setup of promotional materials, books, and DVDs and everything else that you need. Make sure that everything is in place and in order before you execute

Key logistical items that should be completed the night before or the day of the activity include:

•   ˙ making a list of everything you need to do the night before and day of the activity
•   getting the proper address, directions, and contact information

- putting the directions in MapQuest the night before
- making sure the venue is ready
- knowing the correct day and time
- ensuring that any tools you need to execute are ready and available
- doing practice runs prior to execution
- knowing the cost or fees, if applicable

Getting Your Body Right

In order to optimally perform, your body should be in the proper shape. Now, I don't mean you need to have a "Mr. Universe" body-builder shape, but your body should be running in tip-top performance. To be in beast mode, you need to be alert, illness-free, well nourished, hydrated, stress-free, and drug-free. Your body is similar to a car. For a car to run at maximum performance, it needs to have appropriate levels of fuel, oil, water, and air in the tires, with a smooth-running engine and properly running transmission. Likewise, you need to ensure you get adequate rest and proper nutrition and hydration.

Key items to remember to ensure your body is ready to perform include:

- getting proper sleep and rest
- getting proper nutrition
- drinking plenty of water
- exercising
- using stress-relaxation techniques
- ensuring proper medicine is taken
- avoiding alcohol consumption
- avoiding narcotics
- keeping your environment clean and sterile to avoid spreading germs

Getting Your Mind Right

Likewise, you need to prepare your mind to perform. Key items to remember to ensure that your mind is ready include:

- arriving early
- going to the bathroom
- doing stress-relief techniques
- dressing appropriately for the activity

- relaxing, relaxing, relaxing
- focusing on the goal
- practicing your routine continuously
- going over your strategy (how you will execute, how you will respond to the audience, and so on)
- concentrating
- visualizing the activity execution in your mind
- rehearsing in your mind
- closing your eyes
- breathing deeply
- getting rid of nerves
- getting motivated via a prayer, poem, special song, or inspirational quote
- practicing, practicing, practicing

When preparing to execute the activity that day, it is important to follow the three principles above. Being unprepared will often lead to challenging and usually unsuccessful execution results.

Game Time (in the Moment)

This is it! Everything you have done up to this point leads to *now*. This is game time, finishing time, and execution time. This is the most important time in this process. At this point, preparation, planning, strategizing, organizing, and managing your precious time is all in the rear-view mirror. It is time to "put your money where your mouth is." Hopefully, you have the skill to compete, and you have gained the proper knowledge, training, and coaching to put you into beast mode. Execution time is the "truth-telling" pillar. It is time for you to utilize all the information that you have received, gathered, practiced, and rehearsed. This is the time when it all pays off. Nothing else matters from this point except executing to the best of your ability.

The Time Is Now

The key to execution is to handle your nerves, handle the fear, and make sure that the fear and the nervousness do not overtake you. The nervousness people feel before taking a test, making a speech, giving a sales pitch or presentation, or attending a job interview is expected. Prior to the activity, utilize some stress-reduction techniques such as relaxing, breathing, stretching your neck, wiggling your fingers, and getting all that tension out of your body. Think about what you are going to do, whatever it is. Concentrate on the results. You are not up there just to speak, you are not up there just to take a test, you are not up there just to score points in the basketball game, and you are not up there just to run your 5K. You are there to do better than you did before. You are there to do your optimum best. You are there to reach your optimum performance, the very best that you can possibly do with the information that you now have.

Focus on that moment. *This* is the moment—there is no other moment but now, so go for it, get into your zone. Forget about the outside world, and just focus on this opportunity. Focus, and get yourself in the zone right now. Think about how you can drive until completion, making sure you cover all bases. Be thorough. Go for quality and not quantity. It's not how much you say, not how much you do something, but the quality of what you do. Make sure it is correct, and accurate, so you can take pride in your final deliverable. Make sure that you finish, and summarize everything you are trying to do.

Finish Strong

Finish strong by summarizing clearly. Go over the things you just said, and make sure your audience clearly understands the point you are trying to get across. Have that be the thing they feel at the end of your presentation. Likewise, if you are taking a test, finish strong, answer the questions completely, and be clear on those answers. If you are participating in a sport like running a 5K, you don't want to limp to the finish line. You want to finish strongly, and don't leave anything out there. This is your chance—this is your shot!

The Aftermath (Examining the Results)

You've done it! You've completed your activity. After months of preparation, training, practice, hard work, and execution, the journey is finally over. So how did you do? Determine if all your hard work paid off or if you need to go back to the drawing board because you didn't attain your goals.

During the aftermath, determine how well you did against your set goal. Measure those results. If you need to follow up on something after that execution, make sure that you do so. If you need to get feedback on something, make sure you do so that you can take that information and fill in some of the gaps. Filling in those gaps can help you assess how to do better the next time.

A primary goal of EPOP™ is to improve, to do the best that you can possibly do with the resources, skills, and talents that you currently have. There are several ways to gather results:

- test scores
- game scores
- statistics
- benchmarking
- feedback from the audience
- surveys
- polls
- voting
- analysis
- grades
- number of questions asked
- promotional item sales
- improved times
- being hired

Depending on the activity, results can vary in many ways. For example, if you have gotten referrals from a speech or presentation, that gives a subjective clue as to what the audience thought. However, a survey or poll with carefully structured questions will provide a more objective view.

Execute Pillar Final Thoughts

No matter what you do with the other seven pillars, you have to complete this one. After all the preparation leading up to the execution, it is imperative to be mentally and physically ready to go, or optimum performance cannot be reached. To properly execute, you need to control the moment before, during and after the targeted activity. In order to improve, keep monitoring your results until you achieve the expected and desired results.

Conclusion

Being a beast is about being the best you can be in any situation. Take care of what you can control, and the results will follow. It's about putting everything on the line to give the best possible performance you can deliver. From this point on, you will leave no stone unturned, you will dot all the *I*s and cross all the *T*s, and you will maximize and optimize each pillar to ensure you give your all in each and every activity you target. Being an optimal performer is about discovering who you are, knowing what your skill set is, and then taking that skill set to another level.

By injecting EPOP™ into your daily fabric, you will be more prepared, organized, time conscious, knowledgeable, passionate, focused, and ready to execute. You will embrace your strengths and weaknesses while mitigating skill-set gaps by learning techniques, training, education, etc. This understanding of the new beastly you will lead to more powerful, consistent, and effective performances.

The power of passion and focus is now at your fingertips. Learn to use EPOP™ daily so you can discover how to soar beyond your normal, and beyond your good. With EPOP™, you will now be able to understand that top performers finish the race, get results, and make things happen, period. In short, optimum performers execute. So live the EPOP™ way, and unleash the beast in you today.

REFERENCES

Baum, Sandy, and Jennifer Ma. 2007. "Education Pays—The Benefits of Higher Education for Individuals and Society." http://www.collegeboard.com/prod_downloads/about/news_info/trends/ed_pays_2007.pdf

Cimin, Rich. 2008. "Story of Boy Named Tom Brady" *New York Daily News.* http://www.nydailynews.com/sports/football/giants/story-boy-named-tom-brady-article-1.341686

Colvin, Geoffrey. 2006 "Secrets of Greatness: What it takes to be great." *Fortune.* http://archive.fortune.com/magazines/fortune/fortune_archive/2006/10/30/8391794/index.htm.

Ericsson, K. A. 2006. "The influence of experience and deliberate practice on the development of superior expert performance." In *The Cambridge Handbook of Expertise and Expert Performance*, edited by K. A. Ericsson, N. Charness, P. Feltovich, and R. R. Hoffman. 685–706. Cambridge, UK: Cambridge University Press.

FindLaw.com. "What are the Professional Requirements for Becoming a Lawyer?" Last modified 2014. http://hirealawyer.findlaw.com/choosing-the-right-lawyer/what-are-the-professional-requirements-for-becoming-a-lawyer.html.

Hill, Napoleon (1953). Think and Grow Rich. Cleveland, Ohio: The Ralston Publishing Co..

Levin, Heather. 2013 "How to Go Paperless at Home – 11 Tips & Solutions", Money Crashers. http://www.moneycrashers.com/going-paperless-home/#disqus_thread

UW, Green Bay, University of Wisconsin, Green Bay "How can I tell if a website is credible?" Last modified January 14, 2014

https://uknowit.uwgb.edu/page.php?id=30276

Wikipedia.com. "Organizing." Last modified February 1, 2014, http://en.wikipedia. org/wiki/Organizing_(structure).

EPOP™ Quick Reference Sheet

When being good is not good enough and being great is your ultimate goal, then this book was designed with you in mind. The Eight Pillars of Optimum Performance (EPOP™) is a winning performance-enhancement system consisting of eight corresponding performance principles designed to help you reach your maximum potential. These eight principles work together in harmony to help you reach the most comprehensive, continuous, and consistent optimum performance in whatever activity you seek to excel.

Preparation
(Pillar #1)

The first step in achieving optimum performance is to effectively and thoroughly prepare for the targeted activity. Preparation involves developing an end-to-end plan. The plan should identify the five *Ws*: Who, What, Where, When, Why, and How. In order to be adequately prepared, identify, understand, and execute the overall strategy, vision, goals, objectives and actions. The essence of this Preparation Pillar is to plan, organize, manage time, research, set expectations, and become mentally and physically ready.

Skill
(Pillar #2)

This pillar focuses on identifying and understanding your current skill level and ability to perform the targeted activity. In order to optimally perform in any activity, you need to have some level of skill or ability to effectively compete.

Knowledge
(Pillar #3)

The Knowledge Pillar is designed to help you optimize your performance. The primary focus of this pillar will concentrate on how and when to seek more knowledge via education, instruction, training, coaching, tutoring, etc.

Practice
(Pillar #4)

Practice and repetition are the keys to ensuring preparation and knowledge gathering are successful, and that optimum results can be achieved. After you have gained the appropriate knowledge via education, training or instruction, you need to consistently and frequently practice what you've learned.

Communication
(Pillar #5)

The Communication Pillar is the one pillar that binds all the others together. This pillar describes the communication methods and tools needed to optimally perform. Getting clear, concise, and effective information in the most efficient and productive manner is paramount for you to succeed in achieving your goal.

Desire
(Pillar #6)

Of all the EPOP™ pillars, the Desire Pillar is the differentiator. You can prepare all you want. You can get all the proper training or education, and you can practice what you've learned. However, if you don't have the desire to push yourself, the desire to work hard, the desire to go the extra mile, then you will not reach your optimum performance.

Focus
(Pillar #7)

The aim of this pillar is to keep you on track with your goals. With so many distractions around us, staying focused can be a real challenge. Focus is needed to achieve optimum performance and maximum productivity. One of the main reasons people struggle to perform in their business, academic, athletic, professional, and personal endeavors is simply a lack of focus.

Execution
(Pillar #8)

In order to achieve optimum performance in whatever activity you choose, you need to execute the fundamental aspects of these eight pillars. Execution is about the actual doing of the activity. What determines if you will actually reach optimum performance depends on how well you execute. This pillar will provide instruction to get you in a "Finishing", "Get it Done", "Game On" execution mindset.

About the Author

Jeff Freeman, MBA, PMP, is an author and business professional who learned early in life that he could only attain success by performing at peak levels. Throughout his long career in corporate America—including various jobs in engineering, operations, management, project management, and service—Freeman studied how individuals and teams perform in the work environment. His observations eventually led him to create the Eight Pillars of Optimum Performance, a method that consistently reaps optimal results.

Made in the USA
San Bernardino, CA
07 April 2019